CHARLESTON

People, Places and Food

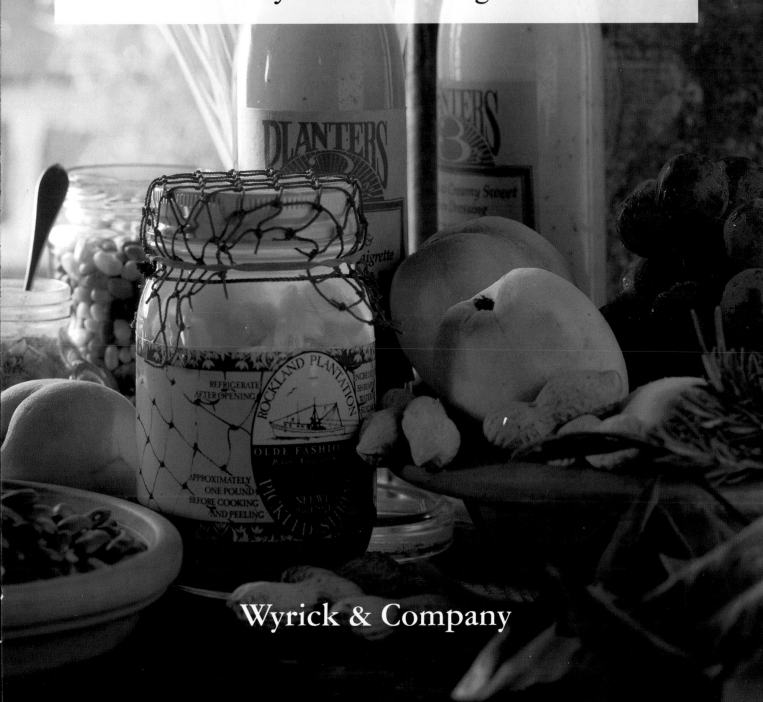

CHARLESTON

People, Places and Food

by Jane Kronsberg

Wyrick & Company

Published by Wyrick & Company,
  P.O. Box 89, Charleston, SC 29402

Conception by L.J. Photography, Inc.
Written by Jane Kronsberg
Photography by Luis Bisschops
Lithography by digital color GmbH
Printed and bound by Printer Portuguesa, Portugal

Library of Congress Cataloging-in-Publication Data

Kronsberg, Jane, 1944-
    Charleston: people, places and food / by Jane Kronsberg
    p. cm.
    Includes index.
    ISBN 0-941711-37-4 (hardcover)
    1. Cookery, American. 2. Cookery--South Carolina--Charleston Region.
    3. Charleston Region (S.C.)--Guidebooks. I. Title.
TX715.K8988 1997
641.59757915--dc21   97-5988
                            CIP

CONTENTS

PREFACE

This book evolved from two who were friends in a previous life
one who loves photography and one who loves food,
both who love the Lowcountry. We have not been objective in any way,
but merely self-indulgent and fanciful because we have that luxury.

The receipts are genuine and very good,
and the photography is spectacular
and gives some peeks into
Lowcountry life sometimes not seen by
the average visitor.

The photographer
prefers to stay in the
background, but it's his
energy and joie de
vivre that got things
going. We have laughed
a lot, fought some and
worked very hard to
come up with a book we
like. We hope our plea-
sure is infectious. Some of our islands have not been included primarily
because they have few, if any, public amenities. Some of the
receipts are included because they fit the photography, and some of the titles
are at the insistence of my friend. If you like the titles, they're mine.

If they don't make any sense at all, they're his. We both sincerely hope that
you will enjoy and use our book.

7

INTRODUCTION

I don't know which I love more, food or Charleston, so I thought I'd do a book about a little bit of both. Like many others before and since, I visited with a friend and knew I had to live here as soon as possible. In those days only a relative few were familiar with Charleston. Our little secret is out now. My thirty-year anniversary of moving here seemed an appropriate time to show appreciation to my adopted city, the grandest of Grande Dames. Charleston and her islands are elegant, weird, and wonderful... just like the food. The "receipts" in this book have come from many sources. A few of our fine restaurants have participated, as have some friends, and I've added a couple of my own. Enjoy!

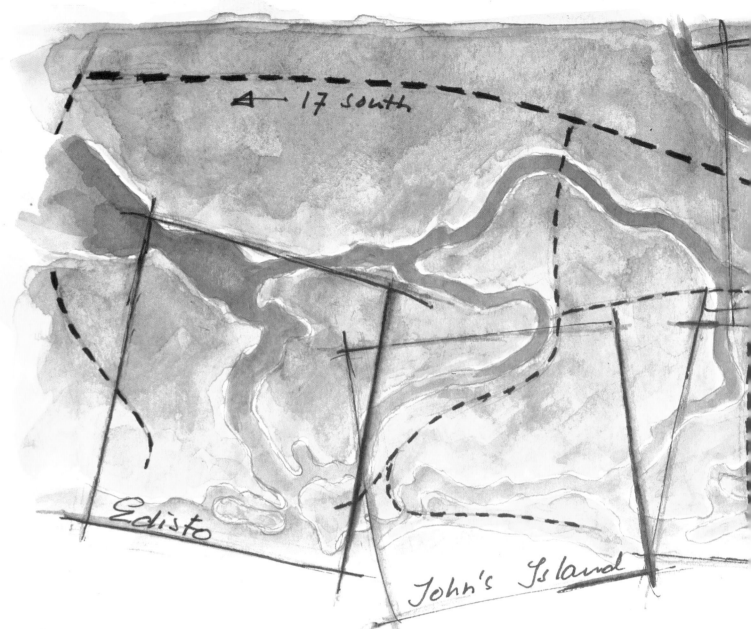

The city of **Charleston** has more charm, beauty, gentility, fine dining, great shopping, good manners and fabulous architecture per square inch than you're likely to find anywhere in America.

Edisto Island is about an hour from the city, but well worth the drive. Marshlands, rivers and beaches give us a reminder of nature's gifts to the Lowcountry. The island has a magic aura that is immediately noticeable and always available to those who are receptive to it.

John's Island is primarily a rural area and is one of our largest barrier islands. Ancient live oaks and incredible marshlands are plentiful, as are pick-up trucks with guns on the racks and dogs in the back. This all co-exists with a beautiful marina and the two well-known resorts of Kiawah and Seabrook Islands.

CHARLESTON   **EDISTO**   **JOHN'S ISLAND**

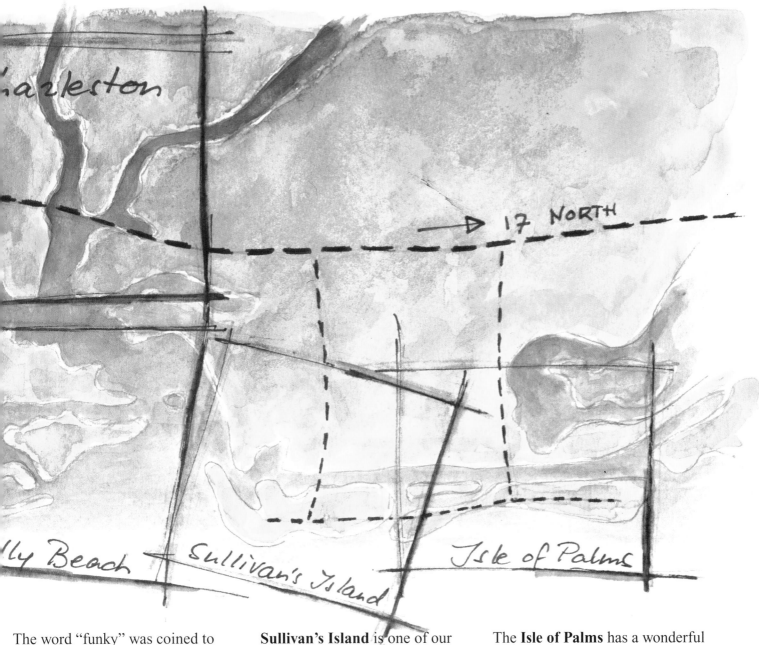

The word "funky" was coined to describe **Folly Beach**. There is a lot of personality and humor here, as well as a fabulous fishing pier, good surfing and always something happening. This thriving community has its own town center and good restaurants. It's close to Charleston, only about fifteen minutes away.

Sullivan's Island is one of our most interesting barrier islands. The many turn-of-the-century structures, a picturesque Coast Guard station, Fort Moultrie and pretty little churches give this island real charm and a sense of place. The island is a family beach with many year-round residents.

The **Isle of Palms** has a wonderful beach and a popular resort called Wild Dunes. Houses with big price tags happily co-exist with more modest beach houses of another era.

FOLLY BEACH   **SULLIVAN'S ISLAND**   **ISLE OF PALMS** 11

CHARLESTON
and the Islands of the Lowcountry

ical fact gives most of us sensory overload. One thing I do know for sure is that Charlestonians are no longer sitting in their dining rooms at 2:00 p.m., having a big "dinner," made by "the cook" and served by "the help". They're all

out working, in aerobics classes or eating at restaurants. They are also not taking tea from silver services at 5:00. I've heard this more times than I can count when I've been on a walk and a carriage has rolled by. With a few exceptions, those days are truly "Gone With The Wind". However, if you're told that people here like their cock-

Here is one of our Southern Belles, ready to take you on a carriage ride and regale you with some history and a lot of rumor and gossip. It's not that she'll mean to deceive you, but only the most astute historians know everything and the gossip is often a lot more interesting. Too much histor-

tails, you can believe it. Many of the old Lowcountry cookbooks have pages and pages of receipts for potent drinks and punches, stirred up and served at the highest social events of the season.

Our state flag is one of the prettiest; who could say otherwise about our native palmetto tree or crescent moon? The carrier Yorktown is also beautiful to some eyes. Boats come in all sizes and shapes in the Lowcountry; there's water, water everywhere. Our Waterfront Park has a fountain

This is the newest park in the city and among the most popular. Going on Sundays is a great time, as folks stroll in their church finery. Also fun is picnicking on the grass, swinging, fishing and boat

a symbol of hospitality and the theme is repeated again and again in Charleston.

The many charming inns and Bed & Breakfasts are a favored destination for many visitors. One can get the feel of the local character and atmosphere

that people just cannot resist getting into, especially when it's ninety in the shade. How many scores of children have come home soaking wet and smiling sheepishly to the shaking heads of mothers?

watching from the pier, staring at the marsh or having a rendezvous in one of the small gardens in the park. This view from the marsh shows the Pineapple Fountain in the background. The pineapple is

when staying in one of these establishments. The standards are high for the many discerning tourists we host now. This was not always the case.

We have a multitude of bridges in Charleston, the longest and largest two joining the peninsula city and the town of Mount Pleasant over the Cooper River. If you want to pose as a native, you must pronounce this bridge and river "Cupper", otherwise everyone will know you're from "off".

This man is dressed in the period regalia that could have had him standing on the steps here at the Old Exchange Building in the 1700s. The dungeon in the bottom of the building has been opened, complete with motorized prisoners.

St. Philip's Episcopal Church is one of the most photographed, for obvious reasons. There is a large graveyard behind it, backing up on the row houses on Queen Street. I used to live in one of them, which had a ghost in my house and one in my back house. My ghost was a woman in a long dress who descended the stairs every day at noon. She lived in the attic and became somewhat agitated when we remodeled the fourth floor. The ghost in the back dressed in knee britches and appeared at the top of the stairs at 5:00 on rainy days. I always thought they could be restless

souls from St. Philip's graveyard.

The Old Slave Mart Museum has been closed for years but is being renovated at the moment. The era of slaves in the Lowcountry is a fact of life, but no one is proud of it. We are proud of our neighborhoods, however. This is one of many gorgeous ones and is

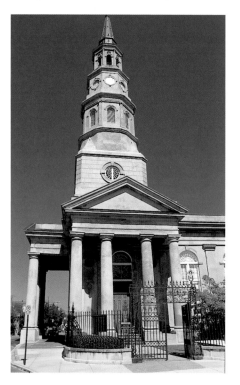

could think of several people who were exactly like the characters portrayed. Nothing is too outlandish in the South, except for poor hospitality and too much complaining.

Plantation is just another word for large farm, but doesn't is sound so much more glamorous?

located in the French Quarter. There are a lot of Secrets of the South, no one but Southerners believe them. I once read a book review by a Northerner about a Southern novel. He said that the writing was good, but the story was just too outlandish and there were no people like those in the book. I had read the book and

Our plantation houses are a cut above the regular farmhouse, and many of these old beauties

remain in the Lowcountry, mostly due to the fact that the horrid Civil War General Sherman and his troops didn't spend much time burning and looting here. Why not is cause for all sorts of speculation, the favorite being that he had a lady-love in the Lowcountry. Besides calling our farms "planta-

tions" we call our porches "piazzas" and our recipes "receipts". Just like the French who have a different word for everything.

Some say that Charlestonians are also a lot like the Chinese because they love to eat rice and worship their ancestors. The plantation kitchen has given us many basics of Southern cooking, but none

reasons; some for pleasure and some for making a living. The shrimpers and fishermen who work the waters around the island have tough lives, but love the freedom of being in the sun and on the sea. There is such a huge demand for seafood, more now than ever

was about 99 cents a pound, but those days are long gone, along with the vendors who used to hawk their shrimp and crabs on the streets of downtown Charleston. In those days before health departments and government regulations the vendors just

more basic than rice. Introduced around 1685, the famous Carolina Gold rice was grown on plantations here for over two centuries. The wealthy planters are the ones who built the great mansions in downtown Charleston, so there is reason for their heirs to worship them.

There is almost nothing more beautiful than a towering ancient oak, but we must have progress, so there are other things on **John's Island** besides oaks, marshes and fields. There are wonderful Mom and Pop vegetable stands, as well as those which are larger and more prosperous operations. Lots of water activity goes on for obvious

before. Most of our prize catch goes to places like the Fulton Fish Market in New York because prices are much better. Thirty years ago the price of shrimp here

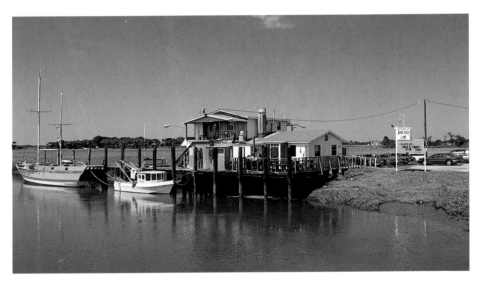

surfers are seen at other beaches, the really serious ones always head for Folly when the surf's up.

The new fishing pier seems miles long and has a gazebo at the end that is fine for avoiding the sun and rain, and is the perfect place for a party at night.

Folly harbors an interesting variety of inhabitants, from old-timers to those who not only remember the sixties, but think they're still here. Tie-dyes, long hair and alternative lifestyles are alive and well.

The new James Island Expressway from peninsula Charleston makes the trip to Folly Beach just a matter of minutes. No wonder it is such a popular place for visitors and residents alike.

back of the island is on the Folly River and lots of folks have great long docks that go out through the marsh to where the water is deep enough for a boat. Sitting on the dock at sunset with a view toward the causeway is truly a fine sight to behold.

Oyster banks are all over the Lowcountry, as are oyster eaters (both animals and people). At Folly and other places you might catch a raccoon savoring the delicacy that thousands line up for at the oyster bar at Grand Central Station in New York.

The lore is that Folly has the best waves of all the beaches in the Lowcountry. Although

rolled their carts around, selling shrimp by the pan. John's Island is one of the few places around here that still allows fireworks, so there are always a few stands open for business.

Folly Beach is a place where "the livin' is easy". This small island is narrow; in some places only wide enough to accommodate a two-lane road and one row of houses on either side. The

Fort
Moultrie
Seacoast Defense
1776-1947

Sullivan's Island is totally charming and a very popular place for families to spend the summer months. Many a small child and new puppy have gotten a first taste of the pleasures of beach living on this island. One of the more beautiful sights used to be that of people riding horseback in the surf at both dawn and dusk. Horses have been banned from the island, and dogs must be leashed when the police are looking, but there is still a wonderful sense of freedom for all. Shorebirds are plentiful, as one would expect, but nearly everyone is taken aback by the flock of mallards currently living at one end of the island. A couple took them in to raise when they were orphaned ducklings, intending to set them free as soon as possible. When the big day arrived, the ducks wouldn't go. They have learned to ride the waves and fly over the surf, but always come back for a stroll on the beach and a word from their master and the fine living at Sullivan's Island. From the beach side, one has a view of shrimping trawlers, as well as the huge container ships that pass by on their way to the port in Charleston. If you watch from the end of the island closest to the city, the ships loom incredibly large and look as

Dunes is on the island's eastern tip, one of three private, gated communities on Charleston's barrier islands.

An interesting mix of stately private homes and simple beach cottages remains on the public parts of the island, and a small town center and boardwalk provide for daily needs and desires. There are several good restaurants around, some with music and dancing, and in the shops we can spend any money we may still have. There is a large marina on the back beach for those with pleasure boats.

though they might run aground. On popular summer holidays such as July 4th the beaches are packed, but generally there is

enough room for everyone, especially in the middle of the island where the beach has become amazingly wide as it steals sand from the eastern tip of the island. The "back beach" is the side that faces the Intracoastal Waterway. Originally called "Long Island", the **Isle of Palms** is another favorite summer place for local residents of the Charleston area. A new development called Wild

ACTIVITIES

Our weather is usually fine enough to allow all kinds of outdoor sports and pleasures. We don't have to worry about icy roads or mounds of snow interfering with our fun. It's nearly a

coming of age ritual for children to be given controls of a boat on an outing with Father. The thrill of handling that ride stays with them always, and one of the first things they ask for is a boat of their own. It's a common sight, seeing teenagers all packed up in a "fishing car", pulling a boat and motor with fishing poles, life jackets and coolers hanging out and a dog or

two riding in the back seat. The dogs pick up the enthusiasm of the children, standing at attention with their heads out of the windows, sniffing the air in barely contained joy over a day in the country with their young masters.

Bikers ride in town or on the beaches, ever mindful of the healthful, non-polluting mode of transportation and exercise. We're more often seeing those on racing bikes, riding for serious sport, fantasizing over the Tour de France.

Many here say they like the beaches better in winter than summer. Not for swimming, of course; only Canadians and others from way off would think it warm enough for that, but there is nothing more exhilarating than a walk on the beach in the wintertime. The magic of negative ions

works then, too. When the weather is warm enough for those of the thickened blood, the water is full of fishermen, sailors, surfers and windsurfers or those who are just out for a casual, noiseless glide through the marshes.

We do the usual, too. Baseball lasts from early spring until as long as everyone can stand the heat and the no-see-ums (gnats

that bite) in the middle of summer. Football begins in the fall, when it's still a little too hot, but we must stick to the national schedule along with everyone else.

Rollerbladers, bikers, joggers and skateboarders can practice nearly all year round and it's not uncommon now to watch a scratch game of street hockey. We've just gotten a new outdoor iceskating rink, so amateur ice hockey is not far behind. Also popular is the sport of parasailing, which by all accounts is a thrilling glide over the water. One can have this experience on the Isle of Palms, but make a reservation. It's a safe and inspiring experience.

Tennis is a sport that is embraced with great enthusiasm in the Lowcountry, among

people of all ages. There are a lot of private and public courts in the Lowcountry, so everyone has a chance to play.

Golfing is extremely popular, too. All the people I know who play just can't wait to hit those courses whether it's raining, gnat season, hot as Hades or cold. Whether you prefer a strenuous sport such as volleyball on the beach or a more sedentary pursuit like sun-bathing, you can enjoy yourself year-round in the Lowcountry.

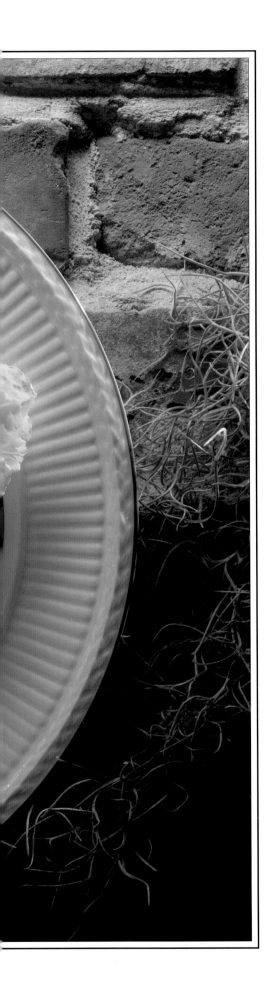

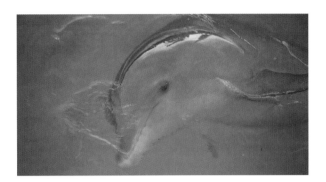

CHARLESTON

"All-America City" does not really describe Charleston, as it's anything but. An honor has been bestowed upon us, however, and we most graciously display the sign. In truth, Charleston is unique among American cities, which is why almost everyone wants to be here. Not to belabor the point, but we have great architecture, a rich history, wonderful restaurants, stimulating cultural events, beautiful beaches and heart-stopping marshes and other natural wonders. We aren't too big or too little, so we have most of the amenities and few of the headaches associated with big city living. Our community is still relatively safe and the historic district is an easy walk. What more could we ask?

Charleston has nurtured many fine cafes and restaurants during the last dozen years because we are fortunate to have a beautiful city that people love to visit. It's been said that we have more good restaurants per capita than any city our size in America.

Although there is a higher concentration in the historic area, there are many very good restaurants in Mt. Pleasant, the beaches, West Ashley and the far reaches of some of our barrier islands. We have everything from one of my favorite seafood places on Shem Creek called "The Wreck" (housed in an old seafood locker with no signs and a lot of "patina") to fine dining recognized by the famed Relais & Chateau. The majority of our restaurants fall somewhere in-between, with many having original, creative foods and ambiance. Interestingly, the cuisine of the Lowcountry is hard to come by in its unadulterated form; it has fallen out of fashion and seems

to be considered too "common" to feature in nice restaurants. Many chefs, however, cook with traditional Lowcountry ingredients and apply "New American" or "fusion" cooking, often coming up with delicious results.

The Pinckney Cafe has been here for several years, serving all kinds of foods and evolving to the type of establishment that never falters. It's a favorite with many locals, and is one of the few places left in Charleston where I will see many people I know. The Cafe is located on Pinckney Street, former site of the Pinckney Mansion. It's

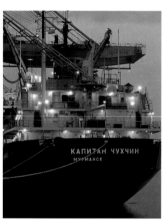

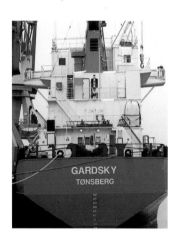

mistress, Eliza Lucas Pinckney, is a well-known historical character who was extremely enterprising for a woman of her time. She cultivated Indigo on a plantation south of Charleston and had a notebook of dozens of receipts that many still refer to today.

We haven't had much outside dining until recently. It's true that the summertime weather is usually too hot for it, but much of the rest of the year is just right. Now there are many attractive courtyards for drinking and dining, such as the one pictured here. We had some spirited public debate over sidewalk dining; it's always fun to watch passers-by, if they have room to pass. People here were having to walk in the streets, which did not work well on some of our busy thoroughfares.

Charleston Place was another source of controversy when the building was proposed. It wasn't as though something wonderful was torn down to make way for it. On the contrary, the hotel was put on a space that was large and empty, save for a few broken-down modern buildings that shopkeepers had abandoned. There was an old Belk's Department Store that had been converted into a nightclub called the Garden & Gun club.

It was originally started as a place for Spoleto performers to gather after hours, and it just took off with the locals. Everybody from debutantes to drag queens went there. We drank beer or wine, danced to disco music and generally had a wonderful

time. When it was proposed that Charleston Place be built there, opposition came from the Garden & Gun Club fans as well as avid preservationists who thought this would be a blight on our cityscape.

By the time it was built, we suddenly had chic international shops and many more tourists in our midst. It was the key to the revitalization of King Street, which, believe me, was pretty dead in those days and needed a big shot in the arm. It's almost hard to believe now, the way King Street used to be. The popular Mills House Hotel, located on the corner of Queen and Meeting Streets was a

broken down flop-house called the St. John's Hotel when I moved here thirty years ago. A boyfriend came to visit and I booked a room for him without looking at it first. There was a hunched-over man who played the part of desk clerk and bell-hop. My friend was dozens of years younger than he and so certainly would not let this poor man carry his bags. When he struggled up to his

room (elevator broken), he beheld a naked light-bulb hanging from the ceiling and a door that was swollen open. Needless to say, I haven't seen hide nor hair of him since! The city's ability to preserve its historic buildings while embracing new ones is the key to its success. The Old and Historic District has special zoning regulations for protection and serves as a model for other cities and historic districts throughout the country.

MAYOR'S MARVELOUS MUFFINS

Like everything else in Charleston, our Mayor Riley is wonderful and aesthetically pleasing. He's been responsible for our controlled growth and has brought a lot of vibrancy to the city. But even the Mayor has to take a break now and then.

BLUEBERRY-LEMON MUFFINS

2 cups all-purpose flour
1/2 cup sugar
2 tsps baking powder
1/4 tsp salt
2 eggs, lightly beaten
4 Tbls unsalted butter,
  melted
3/4 cup milk
1/2 pint blueberries,
  washed and picked over
Zest of 1 lemon
3 Tbls sugar

Here's handsome Joe again, having his marvelous muffins and a cup of good coffee in Washington Park. This beautiful garden is right next to City Hall and provides a respite for overworked city officials as well as tourists and those just out for a walk.

1 Preheat oven to 400°. Combine blueberries with the lemon zest and 3 Tbls. sugar in small bowl and set aside.

2 Sift together dry ingredients in large bowl and set aside.

3 Beat eggs slightly; add milk and cooled, melted butter. Whisk to incorporate. Add the sifted ingredients and stir just until mixed. (Lumps in batter are o.k. If batter is overmixed, muffins will be tough.)

4 Gently fold blueberry mixture into batter. Fill muffin cups 3/4 full and bake 20-25 minutes. Let muffins rest for 5 minutes before removing from pan.

Makes 1 dozen muffins.

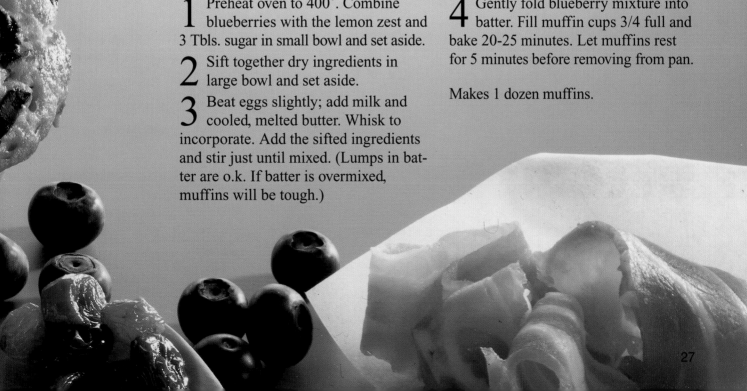

With so much water around, there would naturally be a United States Coast Guard Station in Charleston. Located on the tip of the peninsula on prime real estate, the people assigned to this post must think they've died and gone to heaven. Look at all the smiles!

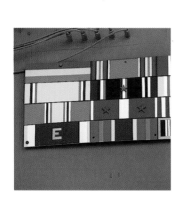

SAVORY BEEF SALAD

Isn't science amazing?! That unappetizing M.R.E. has been transformed into this beautiful salad.

FOR THE SALAD

1 lb roasted beef, cut into cubes (leftovers are fine)

1 lb roasted or boiled potatoes, cut into cubes

2 ripe tomatoes, quartered

1 head romaine lettuce, washed, dried and torn

1 bunch arugula, washed and dried

1/2 lb blanched thin green beans or haricots verts

FOR THE VINAIGRETTE

1 Tbl Dijon mustard

3 Tbl red wine vinegar

2 cloves garlic, crushed

1 Tbl herbes de Provence or 1/2 tsp rosemary, thyme, oregano, basil

Salt and pepper

1/2 cup olive oil

1/2 cup vegetable oil

1 In a small jar, stir together mustard and vinegar. Add crushed garlic and stir again.

2 Add herbs, salt and pepper and stir. Pour olive oil in a thin, steady stream, stopping to stir or shake jar often.

3 Repeat with vegetable oil. Taste and correct seasonings, adding more oil if vinaigrette is too tart. Cap jar and shake well before using.

4 Arrange lettuces on 4 plates, then divide and arrange other ingredients. Drizzle with vinaigrette, but do not toss. Serves 4.

DONALD`S DUCK

*If Charleston were Disney World, Scott and Ruth Fales
could be Donald and Daisy. Our city's not a theme park,
but their food is just ducky.*

FOR THE DUCK ROLLS

1 whole duck
1 cup white vinegar
1 medium onion,
  julienne cut
1/2 cup shredded carrot
1 bunch collards
1 cup vegetable oil
1 cup cornmeal with
  1 Tbl Special Spice
1 cup flour
3 eggs
1/4 cup water

FOR SPECIAL SPICE

4 tsp rubbed sage
1 tsp ground white
  pepper
1 1/8 tsp ground black
  pepper
1 1/8 tsp ground mustard

1 Put the ingredients for the Special Spice in a pot and mix them well. Cut duck in 1/2 and marinate in vinegar and Special Spice overnight.

2 Place duck in roasting pan with wire rack, pour marinade over duck and roast 2 hours on medium heat.

3 Let cool and pick meat off bones, simmer pulled duck in degreased pan drippings for a few minutes. Do not let the duck dry out.

4 Pick as many large collard leaves as you want rolls, shred the rest. Saute the onions and carrots until golden, add the shredded collards, cook another 15 minutes, then add 1/2 cup water, simmer 20 minutes.

5 Mix the duck and collards. Blanch the whole leaves, refresh.

6 Place a small amount of the duck/collard mix in a collard leaf and roll " egg roll style ". Carefully roll in flour, egg wash, then seasoned cornmeal.

7 Fry in enough hot vegetable oil until golden. Serve with blueberry chutney.

Pinckney Cafe and Espresso
Hours
Tuesday ~ Thursday
Lunch 11:30 - 3:00
Dinner 6:00 - 10:00
Friday & Saturday
Lunch 11:30 - 3:00
Dinner 6:00 - 10:00
CLOSED SUNDAY & MONDAY

BLUEBERRY CHUTNEY

8 cups blueberries
8 cloves garlic, minced
2 onions, small dice
2-3 minced serrano or other hot chilis, seeded and minced
2 cups currants
2-2 1/2 cups granulated sugar
2 cups cider vinegar
2" piece fresh ginger, peeled and minced
1 tsp each ground cardamom, cloves, cayenne pepper, and allspice
3 pears, peeled, cored, and minced

1 Rinse and remove the stems of the blueberries. Put the berries, garlic, onion, peppers, currants, 1 1/2 cups of sugar, 1 cup vinegar, the ginger, and the spices in a saucepan.

2 Simmer over medium heat, stirring frequently, until very thick, about 20 minutes.

3 Taste the chutney and add more sugar or vinegar to adjust the balance. Add the pears and simmer an additional 10 minutes.

CHARLESTON

Along with our beautiful birds we have F-16s flying through the clouds. The people at the Charleston Air Force Base are just as nice as everyone else who lives here and handsome, too. Take a look at the major.

AIR FORCE

Major Child is ready for take-off. Could his code name be "Julia"? Air Force is always on his mind.

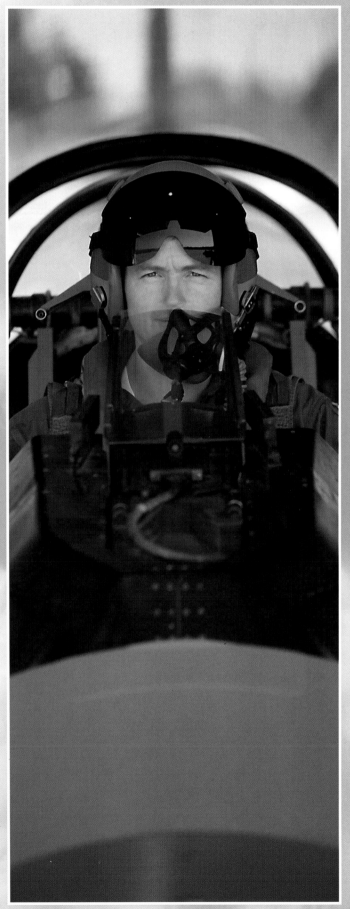

BEANS AND SAUSAGE

8 oz package mixed beans, rinsed and drained

1 1/2 lbs sweet and/or hot sausages (preferably locally made)

2 cups chicken stock or broth

1 lg onion, chopped

4 ribs celery, sliced

1 green bell pepper

1 28 oz can tomatoes (chopped, save juice)

2-3 cloves garlic, crushed

Salt and pepper

Hot sauce to taste

1 Tbl each dried thyme, oregano, basil

1 tsp dried cumin

1 tsp dried coriander

2 bay leaves

1 Tbl vegetable oil

1 Prick sausages with a knife and sauté in stock pot until just brown.

2 Remove sausages, leaving fat in pot. Add onion, celery and bell pepper. Sauté for a few minutes, adding oil if necessary.

3 Add garlic, dry spices and bay leaves. Turn down heat and stir for 1 minute.

4 Add chicken stock and stir. Add beans and enough water to cover. Simmer for about 15 minutes, or until beans are tender but not mushy.

5 Add tomatoes and juice. Cook for 15 minutes.

6 Slice sausages and add to beans. Stir in hot sauce. Serve with rice and a salad. Serves 4.

FREE STYLE FLOUNDER

Do the ladies flounder in the water when this lifeguard's on duty?

TOMATO BAKED FLOUNDER WITH CAPERS

FOR THE MARINADE

1/2 cup dry white wine
1 Tbl olive oil,
juice of 1 lemon,
dash of soy sauce

FOR THE TOMATO MIXTURE

6 cherry tomatoes,
* quartered*
1 glove garlic, minced
1 shallot, minced
1 small red onion, minced
1 dozen capers

2 flounder filets

from The Old Post Office Restaurant, Edisto

1 Marinate tomato mixture for one hour.

2 Take all ingredients and heat in a saucepan on medium heat for five minutes. Preheat oven to 500°.

3 Place flounder filets in a baking dish and season lightly with salt.

4 After the tomato mixture has cooled, pour over the fish and bake until just done—about ten minutes. Serve with herbed rice and fresh sautéed vegetables.

Serves 4.

Julia is training to compete in the summer Olympics. A dish like this "Freestyle Flounder" will keep you in the swim, too.

HERBED FLUFFY RICE

1 tsp each of fresh basil, thyme and oregano

2 Tbls olive oil

1 cup of natural brown rice

2 cups of fresh chicken stock or water

2 tsp sea salt or fresh kosher salt

1 Bring water or stock to a boil. Add rice, herbs, olive oil and salt.

2 Turn down heat and cook, covered, until rice has absorbed water and is soft, about 15 minutes. Add more water or stock if necessary.

Serves 4.

SCALLOPS PIANISSIMO

The famous Dock Street Theater is said to be the oldest in the country. It's the perfect environment for plays, opera and chamber music. Our diva is ready to burst into song—perhaps an aria from Porgy and Bess.

SCALLOPS AND JULIENNED VEGETABLES

1 lb sea scallops

1 cup each julienned celery, carrot, tender leeks (green and white) or shallots

1/2 stick butter

1/2 cup white wine

1/2 cup water or clam broth

1 lemon

3 Tbls fresh tarragon or 1 1/2 Tbls dried

salt and pepper

1/2–3/4 cup heavy cream

3 Tbls all-purpose flour

This dish is elegant, easy and very quick to make. The recipe comes from a friend in France who always has a great table. The cream sauce can be thick or thin, depending on your preference.

1 Put julienned vegetables in a large saucepan or skillet. Add butter, wine and water or clam broth; then tarragon, salt and pepper.

2 Cut out circle of waxed paper and lay on top of vegetables to help them "sweat".

3 Cover and simmer until done but al dente, 10-15 minutes.

4 Quickly sauté scallops over high heat in 3 Tbls. butter. Remove from pan and keep warm. Sprinkle with salt and pepper.

5 Add remaining butter to scallop pan. When butter bubbles, add flour to make a roux. Stir for 3-5 minutes until flour is cooked but not browned.

6 Add some cooking liquid from the vegetables, a little wine if necessary, and finish with cream until a thin sauce is made. Season with salt and more fresh tarragon, if desired.

7 To Assemble: Divide vegetables among plates. Divide sautéed scallops and put over the vegetables. Finish with white sauce, garnish with fresh tarragon.

8 If serving as main course, add roasted new potatoes on the side.

Serves 3 as main course, 6 as first.

CHICKEN ON VACATION

The Old City Market is a most vibrant place, with vendors hawking both old and new. The "basket ladies" skillfully weave the local sweetgrass, keeping alive the ancient art that was brought here from the coast of Africa.

CHICKEN WITH OLIVES AND CAPERS

1 chicken, cut up

2 Tbls each of olive oil and butter

2–3 cloves garlic, crushed

1 large onion, sliced

1/2–1 cup dry white wine

2 Tbls each of basil and thyme

salt and pepper

1 28 oz can tomatoes, chopped

1-1 1/2 cans chicken broth

1 cup green olives with pimientos

1/2 cup capers

Here is the thousandth and one best chicken recipe. Based on a dish from the South of France, it's colorful, flavorful and as easy as can be. You'll think you're on vacation while making this and everyone will love it.

1 Heat olive oil and butter in oven-proof casserole.

2 Sauté chicken pieces until lightly browned.

3 Turn down heat and add crushed garlic and sliced onions, stirring constantly so they do not burn.

4 Add the white wine, basil and thyme. Turn up heat while wine boils down.

5 Lower heat and add chicken broth and canned tomatoes with their juice. If using whole tomatoes, break up with a knife or a spoon.

6 Cover chicken and put in a 350° oven for 1 hour (or 300° for 2 hours).

7 Add olives for last 20 minutes of cooking time. Add capers after chicken is removed from oven. Serve with white rice.

CHARLESTON

Horse-drawn carriages plod along the streets of Charleston, just as they did centuries ago. This can be a pain for the locals who are trying to be on time for an appointment. We try to be gracious and patient; if we're sometimes not, please pardon us.

SWEET APPLE IN A BAG

Horses love apples and sugar, so I thought to cook up a treat for them. The brown bag helps to keep the pie from drying out while the topping happily browns.

APPLE PIE

FOR THE CRUST

1 stick unsalted butter
1 1/4 cups flour
1 Tbl sugar
1 pinch salt
2 Tbl sour cream

FOR THE FILLING

6–7 Granny Smith apples
5 Tbl flour
2 tsp cinnamon
3 Tbl ice water
1 tsp freshly grated nutmeg
1/2 cup sugar

FOR THE TOPPING

1 stick unsalted butter
1 1/2 cups flour
1 1/2 cups sugar
1 cup pecan halves

Makes one pie.

1 For the crust, put ingredients in food processor and work until dough forms a ball. Press dough into a 9 inch pie plate.

2 Peel, core and cut apples into eighths. Put apples into pie shell.

3 Sprinkle with sugar, cinnamon and nutmeg. Tap 5 tablespoons flour out of spoon over apples. Evenly pour the three tablespoons of water over the flour.

4 For the topping, melt butter in saucepan. Add flour and sugar. Mix until soft.

5 With fingers, press mixture on mound of apples until all are covered. Press the pecans into the topping.

6 Put pie into a large brown grocery bag or omit bag and bake in conventional way in 425° oven for about one hour. Crust should be browned and the filling bubbling.

One of the most cheerful carriage drivers in the city tells me that the horses are well taken care of and are rotated regularly, so I shouldn't worry about them. She is the manager for one of the many carriage companies in the city. Thirty years ago there were only two carriages.

EDISTO

Edisto has a rich and varied history, provided in part by the Carolina Gold rice and the fine Sea Island cotton grown there. The cotton was so popular it never went to market; it was purchased before it was planted. Many of the planters became immensely wealthy, building huge estates which included vast formal gardens. Entertaining was lavish, as was life in general. An end of the era of wealth and splendor came when the island was occupied by Federal troops during the Civil War. Those who had been enslaved had an effect on the island's culture, too, and continue the influence today.

Welcome to EDISTO ISLAND
EDISTO CHAMBER OF COMMERCE

The Old Post Office building on Edisto Island houses a fine restaurant of the same name which specializes in indigenous Lowcountry cooking. The interior of the building has been totally renovated, but the outside retains the charm of another decade. People from the island and the mainland flock to enjoy the grits cooked in cream, the fresh seafood served Southern style, the island-grown lettuces and herbs and the mouth-watering house-made desserts.

Below is one of many views of the magnificent marsh on Edisto. They're beautiful any

time of year, whether golden, green or even dead brown or black. There is a certain mystery and aura that clings to these unique patches of seagrass and water,

a certain rhythm that has been there forever. Whatever it is, there's magic.

Many types of long-legged waders inhabit the Lowcountry; egrets, herons, cranes,

and ibises, among others, wade our marshes all year long, looking for supper in the pluff mud. One can nearly always spot an egret in any marsh. About a century ago they

form. There are also rumors of people who can cast "spells" and have the power to cause sickness as well as cure it. Most of those beliefs are gone now, but there are still some threads tied to that distant past.

Another custom that used to be much more common was the placing of favorite foods or objects departed's grave. I have personally seen glasses of iced tea, small tables

and chairs, crockery and eating utensils, cups of coffee and fried chicken on the graves. A very small number of people continue the practice today. Like everyone

elso though, they believe in flowers. The ancient art of weaving baskets with seagrasses from the marsh is a valuable legacy of the African slaves.

Today, the baskets fetch high prices if they are well-woven. The most valuable baskets are those that are rigid and woven so tightly that they are able to hold water. This art has been connected to those who still live on the coast of Africa, in an area called Sierra Leone. Local weavers have visited their distant relations there for an emotional reunion. Amazingly, the baskets are exactly the same as the ones woven here on our sea islands.

That was the key to knowing what part of Africa many of our black citizens came from. It was also a relief to the Africans, knowing that some of their ancestors survived.

became almost extinct as a result of being killed for their plumage. Luckily, they are now protected, both by the Wildlife Department and the dictates of fashion. Luckily for them, baseball caps are in style now. Egrets live in both fresh and salt water, but on this coast they are best known as salt marsh birds.

Many wonderful and colorful traditions and superstitions live on at Edisto. Here are some photos from the lives of those who still inhabit the island. This tree we

found in the marsh was decorated and left with messages; love notes or notes to the spirits, I don't know which. Many people on the island paint their door and window frames bright blue, as superstition dictates that ghosts and other unwanted spirits or "haints" are repelled by the color.

The spirits are said to take many forms, and come out after dark. So an innocent-looking goat or dog could really be the dead who have risen from their graves and taken on another

OYSTERS HOLY MOSES

The New First Baptist Church on Edisto Island was built in 1818 by Hephzibah J. Townsend. She scandalized everyone at the time by attending services with black people. She'd probably spent a lot of boring times in white churches! In 1828, she gave the church to her black friends. She may have gone to the white church pictured below.

FRIED OYSTERS WITH FIRECRACKER SAUCE

1 dozen fresh, shucked oysters
3 cups peanut oil

FOR THE BREADING

1 cup high gluten flour
1/2 cup fine cracker meal
1 Tbl each of salt, black pepper, and paprika
2 tsp of cayenne pepper

FOR THE FIRECRACKER SAUCE

1 Tbl olive oil
1/2 cup finely minced yellow onion
1/2 cup chopped red onion
2 jalapeño peppers chopped with half the seeds
1 red sweet pepper, chopped
1 Tbl fresh chopped parsley
2 cups fresh tomato puree
1 tsp each of salt, sugar, cayenne pepper, and fresh oregano

from The Old Post Office Restaurant

The oysters may be breaded and fried as in the receipt above, or simply served on the half shell as pictured.

1 Sauté all ingredients for the sauce except the puree and seasonings over medium heat until ingredients are tender; add puree and seasonings and simmer on low for about 20 minutes.

2 Heat peanut oil in a heavy skillet to 350°. Mix all ingredients for the breading.

3 Dust the oysters with breading mixture and fry in the hot oil until golden: about 1 1/2 minutes.

SUNSET SOUP

Reminiscent of a glowing island sunset. This soup is rich and comforting.

BUTTERNUT SQUASH SOUP

10 oz butter

2 butternut squash, cut in half lengthwise

1 Bermuda onion, chopped

1 cup flour

1 qt heavy cream

2 qts chicken stock

1 tsp cayenne

1 tsp ground ginger

1 Tbl dark brown sugar

1 tsp ground allspice

2 bay leaves

8 oz sour cream

from Rosebank Farms Cafe, John's Island

1 Spread 2 oz. butter over the four pieces of squash and bake at 350° for 35 minutes until pulp is soft.

2 Melt 6 oz. butter in pot and sauté chopped onion. Dust with the flour and form a thin but dark roux. This will impart a nutty flavor.

3 Add the stock, the dry spices and sugar to the pot and allow to slowly simmer and thicken.

4 Add the chopped squash and cream and simmer for 10 minutes. Purée in a blender or food processor.

5 Use warm stock to thin if necessary and add 1 oz. of butter to enrich the soup. Serve with a dollop of sour cream. Serves 6.

POSTMAN'S PRIDE

There are shrimp and grits, and then there is this—the most heavenly and sinful ever.

SHRIMP AND GRITS WITH MOUSSELINE SAUCE

FOR THE GRITS

1 cup water
1 cup milk
1 cup heavy cream
1 cup melted butter
1 tsp salt
1 cup whole grain grits

FOR THE SAUCE

Juice of 1 lemon
1/2 pound melted butter
4 egg yolks
1/2 cup heavy cream

FOR THE SHRIMP

2 pounds shrimp, peeled and deveined
Butter

from The Old Post Office Restaurant

1 Bring all liquid ingredients and the salt to low boil. Add grits, stirring in slowly on medium to low heat. Stir and watch for 20 minutes, cover and finish in a double boiler at low heat for 30 to 40 minutes.

2 Should grits become too thick, add liquid or butter.

3 For the sauce, whisk lemon juice and butter into egg yolks in a slow steady stream.

4 Add heavy cream. Cook over a double boiler until thick.

5 Sauté the shrimp in butter until just done. Place on grits and top with sauce. Serves 4–6.

Philip Bardin (here with his beautiful legs) has brought Lowcountry receipts to new heights. Besides using indigenous ingredients, he's one of the best fry cooks. Some people just have the touch for what I like to describe as "cosmic frying". If you like his food, send him a card. He's near the Post Office.

This guy had better get his fishing rod if he wants sea trout for supper. But who can blame him for just cruising the marsh, taking in all its splendor?

TAKE A FLY

This receipt is a savory variation on the usual fish stuffed with crab dressing.

SEA TROUT STUFFED WITH CRABMEAT

2 sea trout, cleaned, headed but not fileted or skinned (can use flounder, grouper, etc.)

6 boiled shrimp

4 strips bacon, partially cooked

1/2 cup chopped Spanish olives

salt and pepper

FOR THE STUFFING

1/2 pound boiled shrimp, minced

1/4 pound crabmeat, picked over

1/4 loaf bread, crumbled, including crusts

1/4 bunch parsley, minced

1 egg

1/4 cup butter

1/2 bunch green onions (tops only)

1/4 cup sherry

salt and pepper

1   For the stuffing, mix together bread crumbs, minced shrimp and crabmeat. Add minced parsley.

2   Melt butter in small pan and sauté green onion tops until softened, but not thoroughly cooked. Add sherry and heat for a few seconds.

3   Beat egg and incorporate into mixture, along with salt and pepper to taste.

4   Make slit in back or side of fish and remove bones. Salt and pepper opening, and put in crabmeat stuffing.

5   Top stuffing with 3 whole shrimp, 1/4 cup chopped olives and 2 bacon strips.

6   Place fish in covered pan that has been oiled, and bake at 350° for 15-20 minutes. Check fish—do not overcook.

Serves 2.

BEACH WALKER CHICKEN WINGS

Please don't think of using these cute sandpipers when you think of wings. Actually, their little legs carry them so fast you'd be hard-pressed to catch one. They almost look like cartoon characters scurrying around on those skinny legs, having supper.

FOR THE CHICKEN WINGS

2 dozen chicken wings, disjointed
1 cup butter, melted
1/2 to 1 cup hot sauce, according to taste
vegetable shortening or oil for frying, about 2 cups

FOR THE DRESSING

1 cup mayonnaise
1/2 cup sour cream
3/4 cup crumbled blue cheese
2 Tbls grated onion
1 Tbl lemon juice
2 Tbls minced fresh parsley

1 bunch celery, cleaned and cut into 4 inch pieces.

1 Combine ingredients for the dressing and set aside to let flavors mingle while frying chicken.

2 Heat shortening or oil in large pan (black iron skillet is the very best) and fry the chicken wings in batches for about 6 minutes per batch. Drain on paper towels and keep crisp in low oven.

3 Melt butter in saucepan and season with hot sauce to taste. Just before serving, bathe wings in sauce and put on platter. Garnish with celery and the bowl of blue cheese dressing.

Please don't use these legs either, because they've been walking so long they're tough! Actually, they look pretty good.

BETTER THAN BASIC BEEF STEW

2 Tbls butter
2 Tbls vegetable oil
2 lbs cubed beef (sirloin round or chuck)
6 Tbls flour
1/2 cup brandy
1 cup red wine
3 cups beef stock or broth
2 lg onions, sliced
3 cloves garlic, crushed
1 Tbl each: thyme, oregano, basil, fresh rosemary, ground pepper (or 3 Tbls herbes de Provence)
salt to taste
3 bay leaves
5 ribs celery, thinly sliced
1 Tbl butter
1 lb shiitake mushrooms, cleaned and sliced

Serves 6.

We encountered some shrimpers at another dock who really did look like modern-day pirates. That's how we came up with "Shrimp Bandits". They were a little scary, but not these nice folks here. Shrimpers work very hard, whether or not they resemble bandits. But they love the water and couldn't think of doing anything else.

SHRIMP BANDITS` BEST BEEF

These lovely bandits don't always eat the shrimp; sometimes they just feel like having something different. So, they sell the shrimp and buy beef.

1 Heat vegetable oil and butter in a large pan, pot or Dutch oven.

2 Sauté onions and remove to bowl, leaving fat in the pot.

3 Dredge cubes of beef in flour. Brown beef in batches, being sure not to crowd. Add herbs, salt, pepper and bay leaves. Sauté for one minute.

4 Add brandy and light with a match. When flames subside, slowly add red wine and beef broth, stirring constantly.

5 Add crushed garlic, beef and onions to pan.

6 Cover and cook over low heat for 1 1/2–2 hours, until meat is tender.

7 Sauté mushrooms in 2 Tbls. butter over high heat until just cooked. Add to stew.

8 Sauté celery slices in 1 Tbl. butter until tender but still crisp. Add to stew and serve with rice or egg noodles.

EDISTO SHRIMP CO.™

CHICKEN IN PARADISE

Don't cook this chicken if you're having the Food Police over; it's a wonderful, old-fashioned recipe that people enjoyed before they had so much education about butter and cream.
Try it anyway; you'll love it.

GRANDMOTHER'S CHICKEN

1 whole chicken, rinsed and patted dry, extra fat trimmed

1 cup white wine

1 can chicken broth

1 Vidalia or Wadmalaw sweet onion, peeled and sliced or 6 shallots, peeled and sliced

1/2 stick butter

salt and pepper

1 Tbl tarragon

1/2 pint heavy cream

3-4 Tbls flour

1 Melt 1/4 stick butter in large stock-pot and add whole chicken. Lightly brown on all sides.

2 Add onions or shallots and cook until wilted. Salt and pepper chicken, add wine and let boil down. Add broth and water to nearly cover. Put lid on pot and bake in 350° oven for 1 hour.

3 Remove chicken to platter, slice and keep warm. Reserve cooking liquid.

4 Melt 1/4 stick butter in saucepan and add flour, stirring until incorporated with butter.

5 Cook flour for 3 minutes. Do not let brown. Whisk in small amounts of reserved stock, being careful to not let lumps form.

6 When sauce is still very thick, add cream until desired consistency.

7 Add salt, pepper and tarragon. Let simmer for about 5 minutes, until flavors disperse in sauce.

8 Cover chicken with strained onions or shallots, then with the tarragon sauce. Serve immediately.

George and Pink, a vegetable market on a back road on Edisto, has become an institution. You'll never find a nicer woman than Pink, pictured above with her dog "Beauty". I spied George, peeking out of a doorway, but he didn't want to be in the picture. George and Pink have a huge collection of chickens, roosters, ducks and even a turkey. Pictured here is a rooster whose breed is called a "Frazzle" according to Pink, because the feathers curl backward and look, well, frazzled.

BLUEBERRY BUSTER

The well-dressed ladies of the New First Baptist Church on Edisto talk about its rich history and speak with pride about the recent renovations.

BLUEBERRY COBBLER

| 1/2 cup butter |
| 1 cup sifted flour |
| 1 cup sugar |
| 2 tsps double-acting baking powder |
| 1/8 tsp salt |
| 1 cup milk |
| 4 cups fresh blueberries |

Collections at the church are taken up in locally made sweetgrass baskets. The masters of this ancient weaving technique have their wares on view at the Smithsonian in Washington. The most valuable baskets are tightly woven.

1 Place butter in an 8 x 10 inch baking pan. Place in a warm oven to melt butter. In a bowl, sift together the flour, sugar, baking powder, and salt.

2 Stir in the milk and blend until smooth. Turn into the baking pan, over the melted butter. Add blueberries.

3 Bake in a 375° oven for 40 minutes or until topping is browned and crisp. Serve with ice cream. Serves 6–8.
Note: Try adding the zest of 1 lemon and 1 heaping teaspoon ground cinnamon to the blueberries. Toss until mixed through.

from The Pinckney Cafe, Charleston

JOHN'S ISLAND

If ever one island could be called a micro-cosm of life in the Lowcountry, this is it. Large farms, tomato packing sheds, honky-tonks, plantations, summer camps, roadside vegetable stands, historic settlements, horse farms, resorts, migrant workers, roses, churches, white collars, shacks, golfers, tennis players, Old Guard, tenant farmers and the magnificent tree called the Angel Oak; it's all here on John's Island. Other than all of this, the island has room for great expanses of fields, woods and marshes. There's duck hunting, bird hunting, deer drives, sport fishing, and road kill, so there's always something to eat.

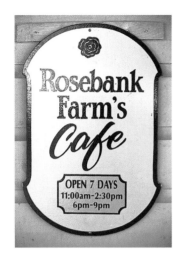

Most of John's Island was "hard-scrabble" in the beginning, providing a life that was difficult and not very prosperous for the majority of its inhabitants. One-room cabins with mud chimneys and small vegetable patches defined the life-styles of many. But Southerners seem to thrive on hardship, whether from s magical sense of optimism or just pure stubbornness worse than a mule, no one knows for sure. But the early inhabitants have perservered, many of their off-spring prosperous and thriving in these times. Not everyone has a boat in the marina or a beach-front house at one of the resorts, but all can enjoy the majesty of the live oaks and the clean-spirit-edness of country living. The sun rises, the rooster crows and all's right in the world.

John's Island has all sorts of things going on other than farming and rural living. This large island is able to support a variety of activities that generally don't bother those other pursuits. The Rosebank Farms Cafe is located at the tip of the island in a place called Bohicket Marina.

Although open for a relatively short time, Rosebank has made quite a reputation for delicious Lowcountry cooking. Every day at lunch there is a "blueplate special" for a most reasonable price, and they offer more modern specials, too. There are other restaurants and shops in the marina, almost all having a splendid view of the sail-boats and the water.

John's Island has a lot of churches all over, these signs pictured being just a sampling. We found that people like to clean their cars as well as their souls. We'd probably be shocked to

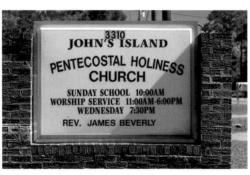

none of the courses is going begging. The waterway from the Bohicket Marina can take you through marshes, past houses and fishing camps, by a seafood-company and on down to Rockville, an old, picturesque settlement on the

know how many golf courses are on John's Island and the resort islands of Kiawah and Seabrook. One course was designed after the famous one in St. Andrews, Scotland and another seaside course hosted the famous Ryder Cup. Some are difficult; others easy; probably some are just right. There are a lot of indigenous golf addicts as well as those from away, so

tip of Wadmalaw Island. Mainly a summer resort, the town of Rockville hosts its famous regatta every year. It's a toss-up,

whether there is more sailing or partying, but everyone has a grand time. Going to the Rockville Regatta is a rite of passage for many young adults.

People who are lucky enough to live or vacation near beaches

take the Loggerhead turtles very seriously. The huge sea turtles religiously return to the place of their birth to lay

their eggs. With the advent and interference of humanity, wildlife officials have had to lend

a hand to ensure that some of the hatchlings make it back to the sea safely. People on the front beach are asked to turn their outside lights off during the season, because the turtles often mistake the lights for the moon, heading to dry land instead of turning back into the ocean. If a turtle lays eggs in a dangerous place, special turtle watchers carefully move the eggs to a safer nest, replacing them in the exact order and direction in which they were found.

GREENS IN ARTICHOKE BOTTOMS

This receipt makes an appetizing and unusual composed salad. Artichokes and tarragon are natural partners that always work together.

ARTICHOKE SALAD

6 cups fresh spinach	1 tsp salt
1 Tbl butter	1/2 tsp pepper
1 8 oz package cream cheese	10-14 artichoke bottoms, canned, frozen, or fresh
1 medium onion, finely chopped	3 Tbls grated Parmesan cheese
1/2 cup mayonnaise	1 Tbl paprika
1 egg	1/2 cup cured olives
1 tsp dried tarragon or 2 Tbls fresh tarragon	1 slivered sweet red pepper

1   Wash spinach and trim stems. Dry in salad spinner. Melt 1 Tbl. butter in large pot and cook spinach until just wilted, about 2 to 3 minutes. Chop spinach.

2   Combine cream cheese, chopped onion, mayonnaise, egg, tarragon, salt and pepper in a bowl. Stir in spinach.

3   Rinse and drain artichoke bottoms, then spoon cheese mixture into the hollows.

4   Sprinkle with Parmesan and paprika. Broil until tops are bubbly, about 5 minutes.

5   Garnish with cured olives and sweet red pepper.

Serves 4.

CRABS ON DUTY

We don't want to say categorically that these guys manning the gates to private resort communities are "crabby," but they can be. Of course, the residents are even crabbier if the "wrong sort" gets through.

Crab and corn soups have been around forever, just like Beethoven's Fifth. Asian cookbooks frequently have a receipt, but this one's good old Southern American.

from The One–Eyed Parrot, Isle of Palms

2 carrots, cleaned, diced
4 ribs celery, diced
1 medium yellow onion, diced
4 ears sweet corn, kernel cut off cob
1/3 cup dry sherry
2 qts crab or seafood stock (can use half clam juice and half chicken broth)
1 tsp salt
1 tsp white pepper
1 tsp sugar
1 pint heavy cream
1/4 cup flour
3 Tbls butter
1/2 lb lump crab meat

1 Sauté diced vegetables in a stockpot with butter. When vegetables are al dente, add flour and cook until a nutty aroma comes from the roux. (Be careful, this burns easily.)

2 Slowly incorporate the sherry, stirring constantly. Add the stock in a steady stream, stirring constantly. Whisk if lumps start to form.

3 Add salt, pepper and sugar, bring to a simmer. Add crab meat and cream. Simmer and reduce until soup reaches desired consistency, about 20 minutes. Correct seasonings to taste. Serves 8 as first course.

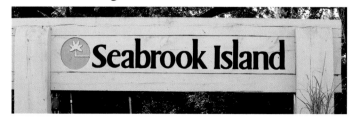

Seabrook Island

TAYLOR-MADE

Casey makes some mean Southern dishes and uses a lot of receipts from his grandmother. When this Taylor works, all is beautifully dressed.

QUAIL AND BEAN SAUCE

FOR THE GRITS

8 cups milk
4 Tbls butter
2 cups coarse, stone
    ground grits
salt and pepper

FOR THE QUAIL

8 quail, partially boned
    and flattened
1/4 cup balsamic vinegar
2 cloves chopped garlic
2 Tbls chopped fresh rose-
    mary
salt and pepper

FOR THE BEAN SAUCE

2 cups cooked sieve beans
    or speckled heart butter
    beans
4 cups demi-glace*
1 tomato, peeled, de-seed-
    ed and finely chopped
1 Portabello mushroom,
    finely diced
2 cloves garlic, chopped
1 Tbl tarragon, chopped
1/2 tsp cracked pepper
    corns
2 Tbls chopped shallots
2 Tbls butter

from Rosebank Farms Cafe

1 Fire your grill. Bring milk and butter to a boil and slowly add the grits, whisking constantly for 10 minutes. Turn down to low heat and cook until creamy and soft.

2 For the quail, put all ingredients in bowl and let quail marinate for about two hours.

3 For the bean sauce, sauté shallots, garlic, peppercorns and mushrooms with one oz. butter.

4 When shallots are translucent add in the demi-glace , tarragon, beans and tomato.

5 Simmer for 10 minutes to infuse the flavors, then fold in the remaining butter.

6 Grill the quail until done, about 20 minutes, turning on all sides. To serve, spoon grits over a platter and arrange quail over. Drizzle sauce over the quail and grits. If grill is not available, brown quail over medium high heat using 1/4 stick of butter and 4 Tbls. cooking oil. Then bake, covered, in a 400° oven for 20 minutes. Serves 4.

Demi-glace is available in specialty food shops.

ROSEBANK FARMS' CAFE

CHICKEN ON FIRE

This fireman and his "Frankentender" are happy that only chicken is on fire today.

2 small chickens (2-2 1/2 lbs), quartered

1 cup olive oil

10 cloves garlic, 4 minced and 6 sliced

Juice of 1 lemon

1 lemon, halved and thinly sliced

3/4 cup cognac

salt and pepper

1 Tbl herbes de Provence

1 cup cured black olives

1 cup Spanish olives

4 sage leaves

Note: Try very hard to find chickens that are locally grown and not full of hormones.

1 Marinate the chicken quarters in a dressing made of the olive oil, lemon juice, minced garlic, cognac, salt, pepper and herbes de Provence. Add the lemon slices, sliced garlic, olives and bay leaves. Cover with plastic wrap and refrigerate overnight, turning the chicken two or three times.

2 Fire up the grill. Drain chicken, reserving the marinade in a saucepan.

3 When coals are ready, grill the chicken for about 25 minutes, turning often. Baste with a little of the marinade, if necessary.

4 When chicken is ready, remove to a platter. Heat the marinade and olives, lemons, etc. Pour over chicken before serving.

Serves 6.

TEACHER'S TENDERLOIN

Everyone must see the Angel Oak on John's Island. This ancient beauty is rumored to be the oldest live oak anywhere. It's breathtaking.

ELEGANT VEAL STEW

2 1/2 lbs veal, cut into cubes	1 dozen pearl onions, peeled and cooked until
2 cans chicken broth, or 4 cups stock	tender in 1 cup saltwater and 2 Tbls butter
1 lg yellow onion, peeled and stuck with 4 cloves	1 Tbl thyme (dried)
	3 Tbls flour
2 bay leaves	1 lemon
	1 egg yolk
	1/2 pint heavy cream
	salt and pepper

What better school trip than being outside with the Angel Oak? The "tenderloins" are admonished not to climb, but it's oh, so tempting. This cool school bus driver is glad to be with them.

1 Lightly boil veal in stock (and a little water if needed) until scum rises to top. Remove scum with a spoon, put in onion stuck with cloves, bay leaves, thyme, salt and pepper. Cook gently for about 1 1/2 hours, until meat is tender but not falling apart.

2 Cook pearl onions and set aside. Keep warm. When veal is done, remove to bowl with slotted spoon. Keep warm.

3 Remove and disard bay leaves and onion stuck with cloves. Strain broth.

4 Melt butter in large pot and add the flour. Cook for 2-3 minutes, stirring constantly so roux doesn't burn. Gradually whisk in broth until sauce is still a little thick.

5 Quickly whisk in the egg yolk and then enough cream to give the sauce a fairly thin consistency.

6 Salt and pepper to taste. Squeeze in lemon juice to taste, about 1/2 lemon. Whisk to incorporate.

7 Add veal and drained onions. Reheat gently and serve over rice with a plain green vegetable, such as steamed asparagus. Serves 4.

Note: If tenderloin is preferred, you can roast it whole and use pan drippings and broth for the sauce. Slice and pour sauce over.

ADAM'S RIBS

Adam is sharing his ribs with Eve. To learn more, read the Old Testament.

FOR THE SPARE RIBS

4 lbs spare ribs
2 onions (sliced)
2 tsp Worcestershire sauce
1 tsp salt
1 tsp paprika
1/2 tsp red pepper
1/2 tsp black pepper
1 tsp chili powder
1/2 cup catsup
1/2 cup water

FOR THE BARBECUE SAUCE

1/4 cup Worcestershire
   sauce
1/4 cup brown sugar
1/4 cup vinegar
1/4 cup water
1 large teaspoon chili
   powder
2 Tbls cracked black pep-
   percorns
Fresh sprigs of rosemary

1 Select meaty spare ribs. Cut into servings or leave uncut. Sprinkle with salt and pepper.

2 Place in roaster and cover with onions. Combine remaining ingredients and pour over meat.

3 Cover and bake in 350° oven about 1 1/2 hours. Baste occasionally, turning spareribs once or twice. Remove cover last 15 minutes to brown ribs.

4 Boil ingredients for sauce until thick. Baste meat before serving. Pass rest of sauce seperately. Garnish with cracked peppercorns and sprigs of rosemary.

Serves 4.

We who live in Charleston nearly forget that everyone does not have beaches. We love them; day or night, summer or winter.

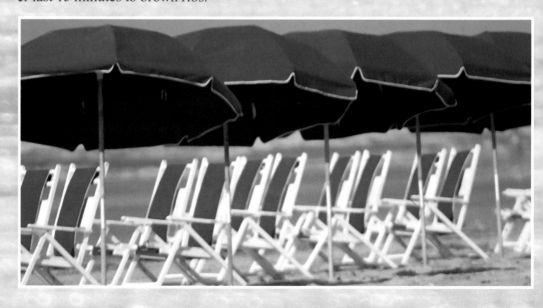

VIXEN'S VEGETABLES

Louise is the talented proprietress of this charming open air vegetable and flower market on John's Island. Her flowers are legendary, especially the roses. Louise and her staff also grow vegetables and herbs, make wreaths and bouquets, and put up vegetables in glass jars that look too pretty to open.

GREEN BEAN AND RADISH SALAD

1 lb fresh, young green
  beans, trimmed
1 bunch fresh dill
1 bunch scallions

FOR THE VINAIGRETTE

1 heaping tsp Dijon
  mustard
1/2 tsp sugar
3 Tbls red wine vinegar
1/2 cup olive oil
salt and pepper
1 dozen radishes
ice water

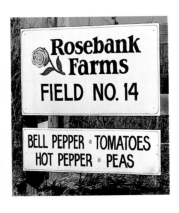

1 Mix mustard and sugar together in a small bowl. Whisk in vinegar, then slowly whisk in oil.

2 Taste. Add more vinegar or oil as necessary. Salt and pepper to taste.

3 Bring 2 quarts of water to a boil. Add beans but do not cover. Cook until al dente, up to 15 minutes.

4 Drain and plunge beans immediatly into bowl of ice water to stop cooking process and retain bright green color. Drain and wrap in dishtowel to absorb any water.

5 Finely slice green tops and white ends of scallions and place in bottom of serving bowl. Snip bunch of dill into bowl with scallions.

6 Add beans to bowl and toss with vinaigrette, being sure to thoroughly mix in scallions and dill. Let rest for about 30 minutes. Beans will discolor slightly.

7 Slice radishes and put in bowl of ice water. Keep in refrigerator until ready to serve salad. Drain and dry radishes, toss into beans and vinaigrette. Serve at once.

Serves 6.

AMERICAN TEA TIME

After using so much energy playing tennis, it's a good idea to sit in the shade for afternoon tea in order to re-fortify for the next set.

1 For pâté de foie, sauté chicken livers in about 2 teaspoons butter. Let the livers stay pink in the middle

2 Add seasonings, then the cognac. Flambé the livers by lighting the cognac and letting cook until flame subsides.

3 Let livers cool, and add all but 1 Tbl. of the softened butter.

4 Remove bay leaves and blend liver, butter and any liquid in a food processor until smooth. Pack into an attractive terrine or serving dish.

5 Melt remaining butter and pour over pâté to keep it from discoloring. Chill for at least two hours, preferably longer.

Serve these pâtés with pepper crackers or thin toasted rounds of baguettes.

FOR THE SHRIMP PASTE

1 medium shallot, minced
1 clove garlic, minced
1 tsp olive oil
2 tsps balsamic vinegar
1 lb fresh shrimp, peeled
1/2 cup fresh tomoto and
*   jalapeño salsa*
2 pounds cream cheese

1 For the shrimp paste, sauté shallots and garlic over low heat in the olive oil; when softened add vinegar, shrimp and salsa. Simmer.

2 When shrimp are just cooked, blend contents of pan with the cream cheese in a food processor. Serve hot as a dip or chill.

FOR THE PÂTÉ DE FOIE

1 pound chicken livers
2 bay leaves
Salt and pepper
1 tsp dried thyme
1/2 cup cognac
1 stick unsalted butter

FOLLY BEACH

Folly is not so named because of an absurdity; rather it comes from the older English definition, when folly meant lush vegetation. Folly Beach does have prolific maritime vegetation as well as the distinction of being the first piece of land assaulted by sea by a force of Union soldiers during the Civil War. They made a big mistake, though, because they could never find a way to get off the island into Charleston! Their efforts at building a causeway failed. Folly also hosted George Gershwin while he composed the famous opera *Porgy & Bess*.

The wacky and always wonderful Folly Beach bills itself as "The Edge of America". Located only fifteen minutes from downtown Charleston, it's the most convenient of our beaches and also the most free-wheeling and interesting. Many who live here are definitely marching to a different drummer. Established as a resort community of well-to-do inhabitants from northern climes and for those around Charleston who could afford a second home at the beach, Folly fell on hard times when devastated by one of our infamous hurricanes. It became, for awhile, a place where few went to vacation, but that is all changing. Bowens Island Restaurant is not actually located on Folly, but on a tiny island right next to it. The restaurant seems a good representative, however, because of its long and eccentric history. It's known throughout the state, and visitors and residents alike go to Bowen's Island for a down and dirty oyster roast. The cinderblock building is located right on the river and the atmosphere encourages "anything goes". Patrons write messages on the walls and furniture with magic markers and staple their calling cards to the ceilings. The ancient juke box plays ancient songs on a wobbly turntable. There is no heat or air conditioning. Everyone who works there has the best disposition imaginable, and everyone who goes there has a great time.

Speaking of writing on walls, how about boats? There is an old boat on the causeway to Folly that is painted and repainted constantly with all kinds of messages. Some of the artists are quite good, others just want to say "Happy Birthday" or "Love & Peace". There are congratulations to newlyweds and those celebrating anniversaries, signs saying "We'll miss you" or "Rhett loves Scarlett", etc. Even lawyers don't take themselves too seriously and might even be

eaten there, but understand it's an old-time diner that is there to sustain with coffee, eggs, grits, hamburgers, grilled cheese and the like. I just love the name and the look of the place. There are plenty of watering holes at Folly, all having a character and personality that is reminiscent of another time and place. The people here have a

casual approach to life, but like most modern Americans, they appreciate good food. Cafe Suzanne and it's sister restaurant, The River Cafe, provide a great combination of new and old American-style cooking in atmospheres that are easy and somewhat eccentric. The scene wouldn't be complete without Captain Harry's bait and tackle shop selling everything but the kitchen sink and dispensing political advice as well. I would guess that the politics would be right-wing, but that has a different meaning in the Lowcountry than it does in most other places. Rightwingers here like to hunt, fish, drink and carouse. These people would seem like wildeyed liberals in other parts of the state. Here they're just known as "good ole boys", which most of them are.

more realistic and honest than most. The law office pictured here has a huge shark emerging from its walls, a fair warning to those who enter. For some reason it reminds me of those boys who used to say "I don't believe in love" right before they tried to throw you down on the sofa. That way, you were

warned and there was no obligation (Sorry to be gender specific, but only women can relate to this). Right down the street from that is City Hall, most likely one of the few city halls in America painted pink with sand dollars imprinted on the walls. Down from that is the Sanitary Cafe. I've never

LIFEGUARD'S LOVE

Even a lifeguard couldn't save these crabs from the pot!
Everyone is in love with him, including himself!

STEAMED BLUE CRABS

2 dozen live blue crabs
3 lemons, cut into eighths
4 bay leaves
2 Tbls black pepper
1 Tbl salt
1 tsp cloves
1 tsp ground ginger
1 tsp cardamom
1/2 tsp allspice
melted butter for crabs

Remember that "If the crabs don't walk to the pot then they ain't worth it." Do not cook any crabs that aren't alive.

1 Bring about 1 quart of water to a boil and add lemons and seasonings. When water returns to boil, add crabs and cover.

2 Let steam for 20-25 minutes or until crabs are orange. Check occasionally to be sure there is enough water in the pot.

3 Cover table with newspaper, supply crab crackers or mallets and a big roll of paper towels. Drain crabs.

4 Have melted butter and a cold beer at each place setting. Enjoy!

Serves 4–6 for starters.

SAILDUCK

Cooking ducks is scary for some. This receipt is fool-proof, and the cooking is done before guests arrive.

FOR THE DUCK

1 Long Island duckling
2 strips bacon
1 tart apple, quartered
heavy duty foil
1 small onion, quartered
1 small orange,
quartered
Seasoned salt, such as
Lawry's®

FOR THE SAUCE

1 stick butter
1 8 oz jar red currant
jelly
3-4 Tbls. Pickapepper®
sauce

FOR THE APPLE RICE

1 1/2 cups cooked white
rice, cooled
1 Granny Smith or other
tart apple, cored and
diced
1 medium diced onion
1 stick butter
salt and pepper
1/2 cup toasted walnuts,
pecans or almonds,
chopped (optional)

Note: This recipe is also wonderful for wild duck.

1 Rinse duck and cut off as much fat as possible. Rub inside of duck with seasoned salt and stuff cavity with onion, apple and orange.

2 Lay bacon on breast in X shape. Wrap duck securely with foil, leaving 2" gap between breast and foil. Place in roasting pan breast up.

3 Roast in 250° oven for 5 1/2 hours. Melt butter and jelly in saucepan. Add Pickapepper to taste.

4 Melt 1/4 stick butter in another pan that will hold rice and sauté onions until almost soft. Add apples and continue to sauté with onions until both are soft.

5 Melt rest of butter in pan, add cooked rice and toss until coated. Add toasted nuts if desired.

6 When ready to serve, cut duck in half, discard stuffing and moisten with bit of sauce. Pass rest of sauce. Serve it with apple rice. Serves 2.

Bowen's Island is located on a little spit of land by the same name. The restaurant has been around forever. Only local seafood is served. The room above is for oyster eaters only. Our friend, Steve, is an expert oyster cooker and never seems to tire of it. As you might imagine, a sense of humor is needed to enjoy Bowen's Island.

HIDDEN TREASURE

Robert's a cooking lawyer. Don't trust him; lawyers are always running after the truth but never find it. But if you find a little crab in your oyster, thank Steve and his dog Ferdinand because they know why oysters look like oysters—and that's the truth.

FOR THE RED SAUCE

catsup

horse radish

lemon juice

Tobasco or other hot
*   sauce*

FOR THE OYSTERS

fresh oysters in shells

1 fire and large grill

2 burlap sacks, soaked
*   (preferably with sea-*
*   water)*

oyster knives and gloves

melted butter

cool water

cold beer

saltines

paper towels

1 Use more catsup than anything else. Adjust ingredients to taste.

2 Heat the grill. Put oysters on the grill and cover them with the wet cloth for about 10 minutes. Have a look at them. If open, remove from heat and serve. If not, continue steaming until they open.

3 Serve the oysters with the red sauce immediately.

Note: Can cook in oven at 425° on cookie sheet covered with a wet dish-towel.

SURF AND TURF

This is a great receipt for crab cakes that are baked instead of fried. If you want to go all out, put the crab into cleaned crab shells like cooks used to do. The presentation is great.

CAROLINA DEVILED CRAB CAKES

2 lbs jumbo lump
   crabmeat
2 lbs claw crabmeat
2 cups mayonnaise
1/2 cup Dijon mustard
juice of 2 lemons
1/4 tsp cayenne pepper
2 cups fresh bread crumbs
1/2 Tbl black pepper
salt to taste
4 egg whites, beaten stiff

from The Old Post Office Restaurant, Edisto

Folly Beach seems to be the best place for surfing because the waves are bigger there. These two boys with boards are just about the cutest surfers I've ever seen. They're good, too.

1 Pick over crabmeat, removing any cartilage or shells.

2 Combine the mayonnaise, mustard, lemon juice, peppers, salt and bread crumbs.

3 Add crabmeat and gently combine, being careful to not break up meat too much.

4 Fold in beaten egg whites until just incorporated. Use 3 oz. ice cream scoop and put on oiled cookie sheets. Flatten gently, if necessary. Bake for 15 minutes in 375° oven.

Makes 40 crabcakes. (This recipe reduces easily to 1/2 or 1/4 for a smaller crowd.)

TENDERLOIN

1 3-4 lb beef tenderloin
6 cloves garlic, peeled and
*   sliced*
1 stick butter
1/4 cup soy sauce

1 Cut small slits in tenderloin and insert garlic slices.

2 Melt butter in small saucepan and add soy sauce. Baste loin liberally with sauce on both sides.

3 Roast at 350° for EXACTLY 17 minutes. Remove from oven, turn, baste. Return to oven for EXACTLY 17 minutes for medium rare or 16 minutes per side for rare. Let roast sit 15 minutes before carving (Meat will continue to cook as it sits). Serves 6-8.

IT'S A LONG WAY TO SATISFACTION

*And then you still might not get it! And when you finally get to the end, look out—
there'll be water and sharks.*

CRAB SALAD SANDWICHES

1 lb crab meat	2 Tbls sour cream
1/2 cup mayonnaise, homemade best but can use regular Hellman's	Fresh baby greens or basil
Zest of 1 lemon; juice of 1/2 lemon	Ripe tomatoes
2 Tbls capers	4 sandwich rolls or bread of your choice
1/2 Tbl black pepper	

Serves 4.

1 Mix mayonnaise, zest of lemon, capers and pepper and sour cream together.

2 Gently fold in crabmeat, taking care not to break up pieces too much.

3 Divide crab on 4 rolls and garnish with tomato and fresh greens or basil.

The fishing pier at Folly Beach is truly spectacular. Sinks and benches are there for the fishermen, as well as mounted rulers so they can't tell fish stories. The covered pavilion is for dancing over the Atlantic Ocean on beautiful, moonlit nights.

SOUTHERN MELODY

I feel it in my blood; it's the tingling in my fingers, the weakness in my knees, the glistening in my eyes. It's Jazz!

JAMBALAYA

*1 1/2 cup raw rice
    (cooked and cooled)*

1 6 oz can tomato paste

1 lg onion, chopped

*1 green bell pepper,
    chopped*

4 green onions, sliced

*1/4-1/2 lb shrimp, peeled
    and deveined*

*1-1 1/2 lb andouille
    sausage*

*1/4 lb cooked ham,
    cubed*

*1/4 lb cooked chicken,
    shredded*

*3 slices bacon or 1/4 cup
    bacon grease*

1 Fry bacon in large pot to render grease. Eat bacon while cooking jambalaya.

2 Add tomato paste and chopped vegetables to the sizzling grease. Stir and cook over medium-high heat for 10 minutes.

3 Add sausages, chicken and ham. Stir and cook for 10 more minutes. Add cooled rice and thoroughly mix with tomato mixture.

4 Cook uncovered over low heat for 1 hour, stirring occasionally. Add shrimp to bottom of pot last 10 minutes of cooking.

5 Toss rice to distribute shrimp before serving.

Serves 6.

This simple Cajun recipe is so easy and most everyone loves it. Andouille sausage is the key. If your grocer doesn't have it, ask your favorite restaurant to order some for you or substitute Cajun seasoning.

HEIKE'S HUSHPUPPIES MAKE ME HAPPY

The legend goes that balls of fried dough were thrown to dogs during dinner to keep them from begging at the table. The treat became known as "hushpuppies".

Hushpuppies could be called "hushpeople," as they keep a hungry crowd calm while waiting for a meal. Traditionally served with fried seafood, the hushpuppy seems to have infinite variations. The receipt here is for a spicy hushpuppy, loaded with lots of goodies.

SPICY HUSHPUPPIES

1 cup flour
1/4 cup sugar
3/4 cup yellow cornmeal
2 Tbls baking powder
dash salt
dash cayenne pepper or
* 1 Tbl finely chopped*
* seeded jalapeños*
1 tsp cumin
1/2 cup corn kernels,
* fresh or frozen*
1 bunch green onions,
* tops chopped*
1 green bell pepper,
* small dice*
1 medium onion, small
* dice*
1 egg, beaten
vegetable oil for frying

Makes 1 dozen.

1. Mix all dry ingredients together, then add vegetables and beaten egg.

2. Let batter rest for at least 1 hour. If too dry, add small amount of water, 1 teaspoonful at a time.

3. Heat oil in stock pot or iron skillet. Put in 1 tablespoonful of batter for each hushpuppy. Do not crowd pan. Cook for 3-5 minutes until golden. Drain on paper towels or brown bags and serve while warm.

CHEF'S BIG LIE

Robert Barber, lawyer and owner of Bowen's Island, is still chasing the truth with this pudding.

BANANA PUDDING

*6-8 bananas, peeled and
   sliced*
*2 pkgs instant vanilla
   pudding*
3 cups milk
2 tsps vanilla extract
1 12 oz carton Cool Whip
*1 8 oz container sour
   cream*
1 box vanilla wafers

1 Mix vanilla pudding with milk. Fold in 1/2 the Cool Whip, all the sour cream and vanilla. Mix thoroughly.

2 Put a layer of vanilla wafers in bottom of serving dish, then a layer of pudding, then layer sliced bananas.

3 Repeat each layer two more times, ending with a thin layer of pudding and a ring of wafers around rim of serving dish. Top with remainder of Cool Whip.

4 Refrigerate at least two hours, until wafers soften and flavors mingle.

Note: Sour cream masks "packaged" taste from pudding and Cool Whip. Also cuts some of the sweetness. Do not omit!

Robert Barber is the owner, chief cook and bottle washer at Bowen's Island. He is a lot of fun and one of the nicest men on any island anywhere.

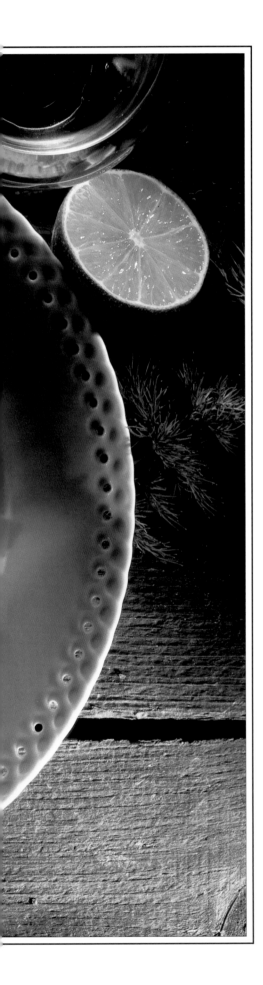

SULLIVAN'S ISLAND

The island was inhabited soon after people came to Charleston, and was named for a Captain Florence O'Sullivan. In 1791, those who wanted to stay on the island for the summer had to pay the state 1¢ a year. The rents have gone up considerably since then! Besides loads of charm, the island has a lot of history: Fort Moultrie saw both Revolutionary and Civil War battles. Osceola's grave is on the island because he died here during his imprisonment.

WELCOME TO SULLIVAN'S ISLAND

SULLIVAN'S ISLAND RESIDENTS
HYDRANT TESTING THIS WEEK
8:00 am - 2:00 am

All of the cross streets on Sullivan's Island are called "stations", as in Station 14, etc. This came about before any bridges were built and people had to come by boat or ferry, then transfer to a trolley that would let them off at each station. When people came for the summer they stayed the entire time and brought everything they needed with them, including livestock.

Everyone had to bring the milk cow and the laying hens and the family pets. Ferries and boats would bring other supplies to the island at regular intervals. Finally the bridges were built and a small grocery store appeared on the island. Still, it wasn't that long ago that vendors would travel in old trucks, going up and down every station hollering, "wedg-a-tables" or "swimps, swimps".

There are no public overnight accommodations on the island now, the residents being touchy about getting too commercial. There used to be some hotels. One large wooden one, com-plete with cupola, was called the Atlantic Beach Hotel, located in an area that was then called Atlanticville, toward the eastern end of the island.

A lot of the architecture on the island could be described as Victorian, although now many modern structures have been built where various hurricanes destroyed the charming old cottages. A lot of ambiance remains, however, and those who are enlightened generally build houses that resemble those of another age. The island has nurtured some fine restaurants, among them one called Station 22, at the address of the same name.

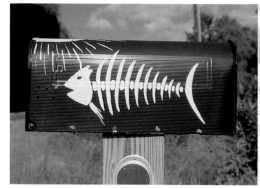

Owned by the mayor of the island, the joke—when he was running for election—was "Please vote for him so he won't have time to run the restaurant and he'll have t

of constricting garmets underneath. The houses on the first and second rows of the beach used to have water under them at high tide, up until the 40s and 50s.

hire a good cook." That's exactly what happened. Now he has someone who is doing wonderful things.

The restaurant has many interesting black and white photographs of past island living, complete with "bathing beauties" covered from head to toe and men in bathing costumes that wore shirts and short pants. Back then, casual wear on a beach porch meant white pants, dark blazer and a bow tie worn with a starched white shirt. Straw hats and leather lace-up shoes completed the picture.

Maybe the good old days were not always so good after all. The women were also decked out; high-necked and long-sleved dresses had corsets and all manner

The beach has built up so much now in most places that high tide is hundreds of feet from the houses. All of the "leftovers" of W.W. II have been converted into

living space. The old enlisted men's quarters is now an apartment building called The Sandpiper. The large, beautiful officers' quarters are private homes. Even the gym has been converted to living quarters, albeit unusual ones. People have built houses under the old bunkers, which provide little light but total protection from hurricanes and insulation

against the heat and cold. Sullivan's Island holds thousands of irreplaceable memories for the families and friends who have spent lazy summer days there. The lifestyles have changed drastically since the island was first settled, but the magic of joyful and uncomplicated times remains. Many Charleston families have had their summer homes on the Island for generations.

STOP AND GO SALAD

When our driver realized we had called on false pretenses—we wanted a photo, not a ride—he couldn't have been more gracious. He stops and goes all day long, and when he gets home his food looks like a stoplight.

TOASTED PECANS AND SOUTHERN COMFORT VINAIGRETTE—STATION 22

FOR THE DRESSING

4 oz cider vinegar

6 oz Southern Comfort

2 oz balsamic vinegar

1 qt vegetable oil

2 Tbls Dijon mustard

1 Tbl honey

4 egg yolks

Kosher salt and pepper to taste

FOR THE SALAD

Mixed baby greens for number being served

1/4 cup pecans per salad

Call Yellow Cab and ask for Charles when you've had too much Southern Comfort Vinaigrette. He'll be glad to bring you home safely.

1 Put egg yolks into a large bowl and whisk in mustard and honey. Whisk in vinegar, salt and pepper.

2 Slowly add oil while whisking constantly. When well incorporated, add the whiskey.

3 Toast pecans, using 1/4 cup per salad (Toast on cookie sheet in 350° oven for about 5 minutes. Cool and break into pieces.)

4 Toss desired amount of salad with a small portion of vinaigrette. Arrange salad on plates and sprinkle 1/4 cup pecan pieces on each.

Makes 2 quarts.

CHICKEN ON TOUR

These bikers on Sullivan's Island are serious and probably wouldn't touch a thing with fat.
The hens provide a tasty, low fat main course that has some pizzazz.

These bikers were out for some good exercise when we stopped them. They were exceptionally nice to accommodate us because their heart rates were up and they were really getting into it. They had to back up and ride several times before we could get the right shot, and they were cheerful about it. The group turned out to be an interesting one. One is a minister, one a physical therapist, one a jet pilot. You're wrong if you think the man is the pilot.

HENS WITH SALSA

1/4 chicken or 1/2
Cornish hen per
person
1 clove garlic per hen,
peeled and quartered
1/2 lemon per hen,
quartered
salt and pepper
kitchen string (optional)

FOR THE SALSA

1 bunch fresh cilantro
1 head elephant garlic
2 lbs purple seedless
grapes, halved
1/3 cup olive oil
1/3 cup balsamic vinegar

1 Preheat oven to 350°. For hens: wash and pat dry. Liberally salt and pepper each cavity and stuff with garlic and lemon. Tie legs together with string if necessary.

2 Place hens in ungreased roasting pan and pour water over until bottom of pan is covered 1/2 inch.

3 Bake hens for 1 hour (a little longer if cooking three or more), basting occasionally.

4 For the salsa, peel enough garlic to taste; chop into fine dice. Add to grapes. *Important note: Must use elephant garlic. Regular is too strong!*

5 Dry cilantro thoroughly and mince in mini-processor if one is available. Otherwise, finely chop with knife. Add to grapes and garlic.

6 Mix together oil and vinegar. Pour over grape mixture and toss. Adjust seasonings if necessary. Let stand at room temperature for at least 1 hour.

7 When hens are cooked, remove from pan and split in half. Put cut sides down on large platter and cover hens with salsa.

Serves 6.

BOUILLABAISSE DU MAIRE

We know the mayor of Sullivan's Island doesn't have worms in his head, but mussels and crab legs instead. Marshall is a great mayor and everyone on the island loves him and his restaurant, Station 22.

3 qts fish stock

1 lb local black grouper

6 soft shell crabs

18 soft shell crayfish

12 mussels or any
   seafood, any amout

1 cup julienned root veg-
   etables such as leeks,
   potatoes, parsnips,
   carrots

FOR THE STOCK

3 Tbls olive oil

1 tsp saffron

1 lg onion, sliced

1 28 oz can tomatoes

1 tsp fennel seeds

1 1/2 tsp thyme

3 bay leaves

4 cups water or clam
   broth

5-6 sprigs fresh parsley
   with stems

rind from 1 orange

2 lbs fish heads and bones

salt and pepper to taste

1 tsp saffron

4 cloves garlic, minced

3 star anise

1 baguette, sliced

1 Heat 3 Tbls. olive oil and sauté onions for a few minutes. Add other stock ingredients and let simmer, covered for 30-40 minutes.

2 Strain broth into clean stockpot. Bring to low boil and simmer vegetables 15 minutes. Add seafood and simmer until just done.

3 To serve, put toasted slice of baguette into each soup bowl. Spoon bouillabaisse into bowls and pass aïoli or rouille and sliced baguette.

Serves 6.

From Station 22 Restaurant

It's fun, looking at the island as it used to be. People who patronize Station 22 donate old photographs of life in those days. The bathing beauties who are covered from head to toe would be shocked at what passes for a bathing costume now, but I'll bet the old guys would love it!

FOR THE AÏOLI

1 lg egg
about 1 cup olive oil (or
  olive and vegetable oil
  combination)
juice of 1 lemon
salt
4 cloves garlic, crushed

1 Put egg in food processor or blender. Slowly add oil in a thin, steady stream.

2 When mayonnaise begins to thicken, add crushed garlic, then lemon juice and salt to taste. If mayonnaise is too thin, add more oil.

FOR THE ROUILLE

1 cup fine bread crumbs
  (dried)
1 small jar pimientos
3 garlic cloves, crushed
olive oil
Tabasco® or other hot
  sauce

1 Combine all in processor or blender and mix into thick paste.

Aïoli or rouille is served by putting a tablespoon or two into the fish soup.

BIG GAME PLATE

If you eat enough of this, you will look like the girls painted on the stern of the boat.

TUNA IN BENNE
SEED CRUST WITH
CHARLESTON HOT
PEPPER GAZPACHO—
STATION 22

FOR THE TUNA

2 eggs
6 2 oz portions yellowfin
   tuna
1 cup benne seeds
   (sesame seeds)
1 cup flour
kosher salt and pepper
   to taste
3 Tbls butter

FOR THE GAZPACHO

3 Tomatillos, diced
2 cherry tomatoes, diced
4 Charleston hot peppers
   (or other hot pepper),
   seeded
1 Tbl yellow onion,
   chopped
1 Tbl rice wine vinegar
1 Tbl extra virgin olive oil
Lemon slices for garnish

1 Combine the ingredients for the gazpacho and let marinate for at least two hours.

2 Beat eggs in dish large enough to hold tuna filets. Combine flour, benne seeds, salt and pepper.

3 Bathe filets in egg wash, then dredge in flour mixture.

4 Melt the butter and sauté filets quickly over high heat, until crusts are browned, about 3 minutes on each side.

5 Serve the tuna with gazpacho relish and garnish with lemon slices.

Serves 6.

Our fisherman is returning with a splendid catch. Yellowfin tuna, seabass, grouper, mahi–mahi (dolphin) and others live in these waters... all hoping the captain won't catch them today.

Windsurfing takes a strong back and lots of stamina. Like many sports that look easy, it definitely is not. Sullivan's Island at Station 29 is the favorite spot.

WAVE ME BABE

After a hard day of windsurfing this tangy pork loin would be just about right. A touch of Central American influence gives this a lot of character. This guy already has it.

PORK LOIN

1 Pork lion
5 bay leaves
3 lg yellow onions, sliced
1 cup low-sodium soy sauce
1 cup vegetable oil
3/4 cup sugar
4 lg cloves garlic, minced
2 inch piece of fresh ginger, peeled and minced
1 Tbl black pepper
1 orange—zest and juice
1/2 cup lemon juice

1 Place pork in large ovenproof casserole with lid. Put the bay leaves on the pork, then the onion slices around it.

2 Mix rest of ingredients for marinade and pour over pork. Marinate at least three hours (better overnight). Turn pork occasionally. Be sure onions are in the marinade.

3 Preheat oven to 350°. Cook pork in the marinade about 3 1/2 hours, depending on size.

4 Remove pork from marinade and slice. Cover with cooked onions and a bit of the marinade to moisten. Put rest of marinade in a gravy bowl. Serve with black beans, yellow rice and a garlicky salad.

Serves 6.

MOONLIGHT SERENADE

This salad is a lot more politically correct than this man is.

Don't let the ingredients in this salad throw you off. This is a receipt from France, so you know it has to be good. The ingredients work together very well and are a foil for some of the natural sweetness that is often present in fruit salads. Prosciutto is a classic with melon.

MELON SALAD WITH PROSCIUTTO

1 cucumber, peeled, seeded, sliced crosswise
1 cup seedless green grapes
2 ripe cantaloupes
1 bunch fresh mint
1 tomato, seeded and cut into strips

FOR VINAIGRETTE

1/4 tsp red pepper (cayenne)
1/2 cup olive oil
3 Tbls lemon juice
3 Tbls heavy cream

8 slices prosciutto
salt and pepper to taste

1 With a melon baller, scoop flesh from cantalopes. If this tool is not available, cut melon into bite-sized cubes. Put melon in large mixing bowl with tomatoes, cucumbers and grapes.

2 Snip mint into bowl with melon, reserving 4 sprigs for garnish.

3 Make vinaigrette with oil, lemon juice and cayenne. Add cream and whisk. Add salt and pepper to taste.

4 Toss melon with vinaigrette. Divide among 4 plates. Put 2 slices prosciutto on each plate and garnish with mint. Serves 4.

SPIKED SHRIMP

If you get permission from the fire department on the island, it's possible to build a fire and cook dinner. All the shrimp on this beach are looking gorgeous and tasting better.

2 dozen jumbo shrimp,
  unpeeled
1/2 cup olive oil
4 Tbls red wine vinegar
3 cloves garlic, minced
1 Tbl oregano
2 Tbls basil
1/2 tsp each, salt and
  pepper
1/2 tsp cayenne pepper or
  1 tsp red pepper flakes

1 Make a marinade of all ingredients except shrimp. Add the shrimp and stir to distribute marinade. Refrigerate for at least one hour, stirring occasionally.

2 Fire up the grill, oiling the rack beforehand. Remove shrimp from marinade and put on rack about 6 inches from fire.

3 Grill for about 7 minutes, brushing with the reserved marinade and turning often.

4 Let cool for a few minutes before serving

Serves 4.

NUTS TO YOU

Peanuts. That's all I can see or think of morning, noon and night. Boiled peanuts. Peanuts for breakfast and lunch. So when I get home, I don't want peanuts anymore; I want pecans!

PECAN RUM PIE

FOR THE CRUST

1 1/2 cups flour
1/4 teaspoon salt
1/2 cup shortening
3-4 Tbls cold water

FOR THE FILLING

3 eggs
1 cup dark corn syrup
1/2 cup brown sugar
4 Tbls butter, melted
1 teaspoon vanilla
1 1/4 cups pecan halves
   or chopped pecans
1.7 ounces (1 mini-
   bottle) dark rum

*from The One–Eyed
Parrot, Isle of Palms*

1 Mix flour and salt. Cut in shortening.

2 Add water slowly until it will hold when pressed into a ball.

3 Roll dough out two inches larger than pan and then crimp the edges. Refrigerate while making filling.

4 Beat eggs until yolks and whites are well blended.

5 Add corn syrup, butter, vanilla, rum and pecans.

6 Mix well, then pour into pie shell. Bake for 15 minutes at 425° then reduce heat to 350° and cook for another 15-20 minutes. Serve with whipped cream.

Serves 8.

ISLE OF PALMS

The development of the Isle of Palms began in the late 1800s with a resort built by Dr. Joseph Lawrence. There was a huge pavilion, dressing rooms for bathers, a restaurant and the Hotel Seashore. There was even a large ferris wheel for the entertainment of young and old alike. Located on the dunes, the wheel afforded a spectacular view of the ocean. There were still no bridges to this barrier island; vacationers rode the trolley from Sullivan's Island, over trestles across Breach Inlet to the Isle of Palms. All remains of the glorious former resort have long since vanished, but vacationers and residents enjoy many new amenities today.

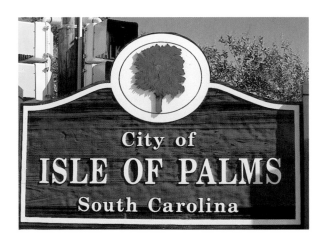

City of
ISLE OF PALMS
South Carolina

The Isle of Palms has reclaimed its resort status with the development of Wild Dunes, on the eastern tip of the island. Unlike its former counterpart, the resort is not open to the public and one must pass muster through the guarded entrance. However, there is an abundance of public life on the rest of the island, with access to beautiful wide beaches and lots of amenities for those wishing to visit for the day. The One-Eyed Parrot and Banana Cabana offer all sorts of refreshment and sustenance, as do several of the other popular spots on the front beach. A relative new addition of a sushi bar makes sense for those who prefer a light meal in the middle of a sultry day at the beach. The Windjammer provides fun at night for beachgoers who love to dance. It, too, is located on the front beach. Although the Isle of Palms is traditionally a family beach, the inhabitants there have been more welcoming to "day-trippers" and those looking for entertainment than neighboring Sullivan's Island. There are public parking and restrooms, beach shops, ice cream parlors and snack stands.

The inlet that separates the Isle of Palms and Sullivan's Island is a small body of water-spanned by a short bridge. It looks harmless enough, but it is treacherous. Although it is perfectly fun and safe to fish from the bridge and the seashore beneath it, the currents are swift and deadly. Many have lost their lives there. Most people who live in the Charleston area learn great respect for the water at an early age. We teach our children to swim as soon as possible, all the while letting them know the water is just as dangerous as it is fun. Many signs are posted at Breach Inlet,

letting people know they should not swim there.

Unfortunately, some do, mostly visitors who just don't understand

that's why I want to go."

On a brighter note, the rest of the Island is perfectly safe, offering miles of wide beaches to enjoy at any time of year. The back beach, or side facing the Intracoastal Waterway, has wonderful marsh views and access to deep water. Many living on this side have long docks spilling out over the marshes. All sorts of boats are tied up, from sleek boats anyone

would envy to home-made house or "party" boats, complete with wide decks and vast canopies, ready for a relaxing evening cruise with friends.

Hurricane Hugo hit the island hard, and many of the older beach cottages have been

replaced with imposing new structures. A new connector from Highway 17 not only cuts the time getting to the island, but provides a safe, modern evacuation route if one of Hugo's cousins should decide to visit in the future.

the dangers, and who are additionally stubborn as mules, like those macho, "sportive" European men who have to take risks in order to prove their manhood. Although this seems to be a particular affliction of the French, I've learned that Dutch people are just as bad. One said to me not long ago, "I want to go swimming here." I pointed out the sign, told him the horrible stories, etc., and all he said was, "Yes,

COP'S CONDITIONER

This is the guy who keeps giving me all the tickets. He's a great policeman, but loves his job too much (or maybe it's me).

FOR THE SALAD

4 cups mesclun, cleaned
2 red Bartlett pears
1/2 cup walnuts, chopped
1/4 lb Clemson Blue cheese, crumbled

FOR THE DRESSING

1 cup walnut oil
1/4 cup cider vinegar
1/4 cup fresh squeezed orange juice
2 Tbls poppy seeds
salt and pepper to taste

Serves 4.

from The Pinckney Cafe, Charleston

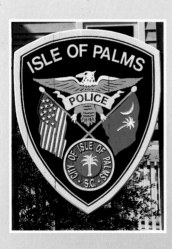

1 Place 1 cup of greens on serving plate. Slice pears thin and arrange 1/2 pear on each salad.

2 Sprinkle 1 Tbl. walnuts and 2 Tbls. crumbled blue cheese. Drizzle with poppy seed dressing.

This is a refreshing, beautiful salad to enjoy anytime of year—July 4th, Christmas or October 22nd. The blue cheese from Clemson, South Carolina is the best. The Charleston City Police come to the Isle of Palms just to have it.

SPORTSMEN`S SURPRISE

Pâté is right with a good glass of red wine after a hard day of surf fishing and hanging out at the beach.

This is a good pâté that can be either served from its terrine or unmolded and sliced. This makes a lot, but men love it so there may not be much left. Keeps refrigerated for about 2 weeks. Freezing doesn't affect the taste, but pâté will be crumbly.

COUNTRY PÂTÉ

1/2 lb calves' liver, ground
1 1/2 lbs pork, ground
1/2 lb pork fat, ground
1/2 lb veal, ground
1 lb pork fat, sliced thin
1 clove garlic, minced
2 tsps lemon juice
2 eggs, beaten
1 bunch scallions, sliced
3 Tbls butter
3 Tbls flour
3 Tbls cream
2 Tbls salt
1 Tbl pepper
1 tsp allspice
1 cup brandy or cognac
3 bay leaves

Note: If sliced pork fat is not available, use thin strips of fat bacon.

1 Have butcher grind meats. Mix together in a large bowl. Melt butter in skillet and cook scallions until soft. Stir in garlic and cook for 30 sec. Empty pan into meat and stir.

2 Add eggs, salt, pepper, allspice, lemon juice, flour and cream to meat. Stir to mix well. Pour brandy in skillet and boil over high heat for one minute. Add to meat mixture.

3 Line terrine with strips of fat on bottom and sides. Make strips on sides long enough to fit over top of pâté.

4 Fill terrine with pâté. Cover and seal with pork fat, using little pieces to cover any cracks.

5 Lay the 3 bay leaves on top of the fat. Cover terrine tightly with foil, then cover with lid if one is available.

6 Preheat oven to 350°. Put terrine in a pan large enough to hold it and about 3 inches of boiling water. Put pan in oven and cook for 2 hours.

7 Remove pan from water bath and let cool for at least 1 hour. Remove foil and replace with fresh piece.

8 Weight terrine so that meat will cool in fat. Keep weights on while refrigerating overnight (A couple of days even better). Serve with crackers or toasted baguette rounds. Have cornichons and Dijon mustard on hand.

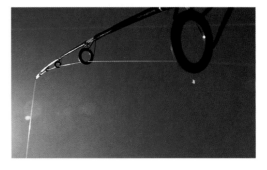

ONE-EYED DOLPHIN

Chad of the One-Eyed Parrot serves his dolphin to Steve, manager of the Parrot and the Banana Cabana. Man with knees in his shirt is the chef for the Cabana.

PARADISE–STYLE DOLPHIN

8 oz dolphin filet or other fish, broiled, grilled or sautéed

CARAMELIZED ONION

1/2 red onion
1/4 cup sugar
3 Tbls lemon juice

TOPPING FOR FISH

1/4 cup each, chopped: Vidalia onion, yellow pepper, red pepper, cucumber, carrot, celery
1/4 cup tomato paste
1/4 cup shredded Monterey Jack Cheese
salt & pepper to taste
1 clove garlic, thinly sliced
1 Tbl filé powder
1 lemon, thinly sliced
cilantro

1 Sauté red onion until translucent.

2 Add lemon juice to deglaze pan, then add the sugar and simmer for about three minutes. Set aside.

3 For the fish topping, sauté the chopped vegetables with the garlic until the Vidalia onion is translucent.

4 Stir in tomato paste. Spread mixture on top of filet, top with shredded cheese and broil for a minute or two until melted and lightly browned. Set aside.

5 Arrange caramelized onions on plate and place filet on top. Garnish fish with thinly sliced lemons and chopped cilantro.

from the One-Eyed Parrot, Isle of Palms

Right on the ocean, the One–Eyed Parrot and the Banana Cabana are fun places. One's upstairs, one's down. Both serve great food.

EN GARDE

The reel is upside down, but maybe the fish won't notice. If you don't have fresh ingredients, turn to another page.

FOR THE SALSA

1 bunch cilantro, minced
4 vine-ripened tomatoes, small dice
1 Vidalia or Wadmalaw sweet onion, small dice
1 1/2 tsps cumin
1 tsp coriander
olive oil
salt

FOR THE FISH

4 portions swordfish steaks (about 1/2 pound each)
1 bunch parsley, minced
1 bunch cilantro, minced
2 Tbls olive oil
salt and pepper
2 limes, quartered for garnish

Serves 4.

1 Put diced ripe tomatoes, diced onion, minced cilantro, cumin and coriander in a bowl and mix thoroughly.

2 Add about 2 Tbls. olive oil and salt to taste. Cover and let the flavors mingle for at least 1 hour. Refrigerate if keeping longer, allowing salsa to come to room temperature before serving with fish.

Note: This salsa is great with tortilla chips, too. If vine-ripened tomatoes are not available, do not make it.

3 Pre-heat broiler or start grill. Trim swordfish steaks of any dark meat.

4 Mix together minced parsley and cilantro. Bind with about 1/3 cup olive oil and salt and pepper mixture liberally.

5 Press herbs into both sides of fish steaks and let rest at least 20 minutes (longer is better).

6 Broil or grill fish. Do not overcook! Garnish with 1/2 cup salsa and 2 lime wedges.

The swords can be polished and worked like scrimshaw or left natural and used as a casual decoration. These swords could become the next hot thing at flea markets, so don't throw them away!

FLY, FLY AWAY

Is anything more exhilarating than kites at the beach on a sunny day?
Yes, but we can't talk about that here.

SQUAB WITH WILD BLUEBERRY SAUCE

FOR THE SQUAB

6 squab breasts
kosher salt
black pepper, freshly
* ground*

FOR THE SAUCE

pan drippings from the
* squab*
1 Tbl port wine
1/2 cup chicken stock
kosher salt and pepper to
* taste*
3/4 cup wild blueberrries

FOR THE HASH

3 Idaho potatoes, diced
3/4 cup green beans
1/4 cup red onions, diced
1/4 cup yellow peppers,
* diced*
2 Tbls Poblano chilies,
* diced*
1 rib celery, diced
1/2 parsnip, diced
3 Tbls butter

from Station 22
Restaurant, Sullivan's
Island

Another fowl could be
substituted for squab:
duck, Cornish hen or
chicken breasts, for
example. The vegetable
hash and blueberry
gravy make this a deli-
cious departure from the
usual.

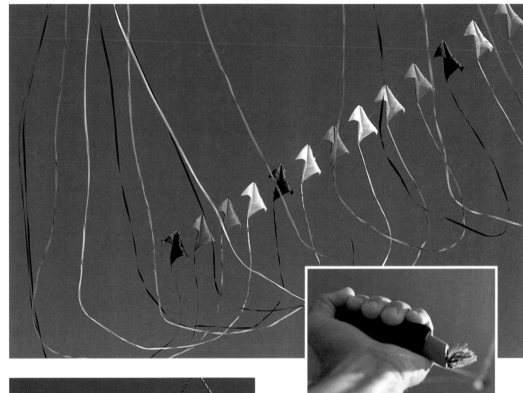

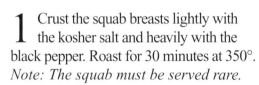

1 Crust the squab breasts lightly with the kosher salt and heavily with the black pepper. Roast for 30 minutes at 350°. *Note: The squab must be served rare.*

2 Reserve the pan drippings from the roasted squab for the blueberry pan gravy.

3 Combine sauce ingredients and whisk until blended well. Add blueberries. Heat until warm, but not boiling.

4 Melt 3-4 Tbls. butter in a large pan. Add hash ingredients and stir-fry until al dente, about 10 minutes.

5 To serve, place hash on a platter. Fan sliced breast on vegetables, and moisten with small amount of blueberry gravy. Pass rest of gravy separately. Serves 4.

EASY SOUND

This looks a little more frenetic than the usual serenade, but hey, it's the end of the millenium and things have changed. Hopefully, "You Light Up My Life" will be banned in the next century.

BLACK BEANS

*1 lb black beans, washed
    and soaked*
1 medium onion, chopped
*1 green bell pepper,
    chopped*
2 Tbls olive oil
3 bay leaves
1 can chicken broth
1 Tbl coriander
1 Tbl oregano

FOR THE SALSA

*1 small onion, finely
    chopped*
1 tomato, diced
2 cloves garlic, crushed
1/4 cup minced parsley
1/4 cup olive oil
2 Tbls red wine vinegar
1 1/2 tsp cumin
sour cream (optional)

Serves 6.

If you are not ready to tear your hair out over yet another black bean, remember that they're both tasty and nutritious. These don't need the traditional raw onion and chopped egg garnish, only yellow or white rice and a crispy romaine salad with lots of garlic in the dressing. The beans have lots of protein, so hold the beef.

1 Heat 2 Tbls. olive oil in a large pot. Sauté onions and bell pepper for a few minutes.

2 Add bay leaves, coriander, oregano, beans, chicken stock and water. Cover and cook over low until tender, about 1 1/2 hours.

3 While beans are cooking, mix salsa and let stand.

4 Remove 1 cup of beans and mash with fork, then return to pot and stir.

5 Stir salsa into beans just before serving. Garnish with sour cream.

DIZZY SEAFOOD

Another day in the life of the Lowcountry, riding the seas in a big boat, getting lots of sunshine and fresh air, chatting with friends and looking forward to a delicious meal when returning home. I don't know how we make these sacrifices, but Southerners are known to be a sturdy and uncomplaining lot.

2 dozen mussels, cleaned
1 dozen clams, cleaned
2 dozen jumbo shrimp, heads and shells on
8 crab claws (optional)

or any combination of above

1/2 cup olive oil
2 hot peppers, seeded and sliced, or 1 tsp red pepper flakes
8 cloves garlic, 4 minced and 4 diced
1 ripe tomato, seeded and chopped or one 14 oz can diced tomatoes
1 1/2 cups dry champagne
salt and pepper to taste
5 Tbls chopped fresh parsley
4 Tbls chopped fresh tarragon or basil

1 Heat olive oil in large pot or Dutch oven over medium heat. Sauté hot peppers for about one minute; then add minced and diced garlic for about 30 seconds, being careful not to burn.

2 Add the tomatoes and champagne and bring to a boil. Add the mussels, clams, and crab legs. Reduce heat and simmer for about 6 minutes. Add the shrimp and simmer for 3 or 4 more minutes, or until shrimp turns pink and shellfish open. Sprinkle the seafood with the chopped parsley and tarragon or basil. *(Note: For a Thai taste, use chopped mint and cilantro instead of other fresh herbs.)*

3 Serve immediately in shallow soup bowls with the broth and lots of crusty French bread.

Serves 4.

FROZEN DREAMS

It didn't take too much coaxing to get these boys to pose, especially when we said,
"The ice cream's on us"!

LEMON MILK SORBET

1 qt whole milk
juice of 5 lemons
zest of 2 lemons
1 cup sugar
1/4 cup heavy cream

1 Scald the milk and freeze in shallow bowl until it forms a crust. Stir in lemon juice, zest and sugar.

2 Put back in freezer and stir about every half hour as it freezes to insure a smooth texture.

3 Fold in the cream after the first stirring. Let soften a bit in the refrigerator before serving.

Makes one generous quart.

INDEX

RECIPES BY CATEGORY

SPECIAL THANKS

To all of you who just let us barge in unannounced, a special thank you for being so gracious,
trusting and understanding. It's true, I was locked in a cage for a few minutes when we went to photograph
the jet pilot, with Luis hollering in the background "Tell them I'm not German, give them my Dutch passport",
but once it was determined that we were working on a book, they couldn't have been nicer.
We had to go through some red tape at the Coast Guard Station but they, too, welcomed us and let us on their
buoy tender. We went to a church service at the New First Baptist Church on Edisto,
and we got the mayor of Charleston to sit with us in Washington Park.
We talked and laughed with all kinds of people, getting to know them and finding out about their lives and work.
It was a very enriching experience and I thank all of you for that.

Thanks, too, to the participating restaurants who gave us their secrets and their time,
never grumbling when we showed up with cameras and notepads just one more time. The chefs
were especially nice when I bothered them during the dinner hour. I made a special effort not to arrive then,
knowing they'd be busy; but often it would be the only time they could be reached.

Thanks to my husband and son for having to either listen to me or be ignored,
whatever was happening that day. My friends have been very supportive, cheerleading me along the way.
Wyrick and Company deserves special kudos for being so patient with this novice who was constantly
late with copy and constantly interrupting the routine. Thanks to Luis for giving me this opportunity
and for not holding it against me when I would get into a snit.
(Even though it was always his fault!)